purch. at Dollar
Tree in Lansing
on Thurs. May 13/2010
@$1.00

cpyrgt 2008.

THE FALL
OF THE EVANGELICAL
NATION

THE FALL
OF THE EVANGELICAL
NATION

*The Surprising Crisis
Inside the Church*

CHRISTINE WICKER

HarperOne
An Imprint of HarperCollins*Publishers*

HarperOne

HarperCollins books may be purchased for educational, business, or sales promotional use. For information please write: Special Markets Department, HarperCollins Publishers, 10 East 53rd Street, New York, NY 10022.

HarperCollins Web site: http://www.harpercollins.com
HarperCollins®, ⏚®, and HarperOne™ are
trademarks of HarperCollins Publishers

FIRST EDITION

Designed by Level C

Library of Congress Cataloging-in-Publication Data

Wicker, Christine.
The fall of the evangelical nation : the surprising crisis inside the church /
Christine Wicker. — 1st ed.
p. cm.
ISBN 978–0–06–111716–9
1. Evangelicalism—United States.   2. United States—Church history—21st century.
I. Title.
BR1642.U5W53   2008
280'.40973—dc22   2008006584

08 09 10 11 12 RRD(H) 10 9 8 7 6 5 4 3 2 1

To my sister, Jamie

CONTENTS

"duping" } a person easily
tricked or fooled ... to
deceive by trickery ....

Contents

Part Two
THREATS INSIDE THE EVANGELICAL CHURCH

Part Three
THREATS OUTSIDE THE EVANGELICAL CHURCH

(no glossary in here)

Август 2008...

(6 pp.)

INTRODUCTION *– goes to pg. XIV...*

Evangelical Christianity in America is dying. The great evangelical movements of today are not a vanguard. They are a remnant, unraveling at every edge. Look at it any way you like: Conversions. Baptisms. Membership. Retention. Participation. Giving. Attendance. Religious literacy. Effect on the culture. All are down and dropping. It's no secret. Even as evangelical forces trumpet their purported political and social victories, insiders are anguishing about their great losses, fearing what the future holds. Nobody knows what to do about it. A lot of people can't believe it. No wonder. The idea that evangelicals are taking over America is one of the greatest publicity scams in history, a perfect coup accomplished by savvy politicos and religious leaders, who understand media weaknesses and exploit them brilliantly.

I'm a religion reporter, which means I should have known long ago. I suspected, but there was so much hubbub, so much fanfare, and the evangelical story was so rich, so full of nuts and cranks and powermongers, scandals, outlandish tales, and heartfelt stories of amazing faith. On the surface, their story was rock solid. Evangelicals are great communicators, well organized, and in control of amazing publicity machines. Besides that, they're fierce fighters with a persecution complex that won't quit and a hefty sense of righteousness behind it. Challenge their holiness too much, cover their enemies too favorably, and you're likely to have a screaming, kicking, send-you-straight-to-hell battle on your hands. Insiders hinted that the ranks of evangelicalism were not as robust as everyone thought they were. I'd heard that before, but nobody had numbers. It was just a comment here and a suggestion there. Some preachers were sounding alarms, but they didn't get much press. When hadn't preachers been lamenting something or other? Pronouncements of impending doom abound within evangelical ranks. They always have.

Having been saved at the age of nine in an Oklahoma City Southern Baptist church, coming from a family that's been evangelical for at least four generations, I know more about Bible-based faith than most people do. I know the faults of it inside out. A child's open heart is easy tender for the fiery sermons of evangelical preachers. A thousand righteous conflagrations have burned in mine, leaving behind a residue of guilt, shame, and perfectionism that none of my reclamation efforts has quite cleaned up. I have some of the purging fury that child-converts-turned-apostates use to protect themselves, and I have the despair that goes with it.

I also know the strengths and glories of evangelical faith, and that story wasn't being told. The loud, cocksure, flamboyant, sometimes ridiculous evangelicals whose tales make it into the national press are only a small part of the reality. So a few years ago I returned to a Southern Baptist church in Texas for a second look at the faith of my youth. My objective was to see if the kindness I remembered, the humility, the questioning, the ready laughter, the sincerity, were still there. I set out to see if evangelicals still struggle to be tolerant and loving while bound by implacable rules, those edicts handed down by Almighty God himself that define their faith. I wanted to explain why so many people cling to evangelical faith. I wanted to illustrate the magnificence it can have, the community it can create.

My destination was an evangelical megachurch of local renown near Dallas, because I practiced evangelical faith and left it while growing up near Dallas. I also picked Dallas because it's got more evangelicals per square inch than any other place in the world. Why a megachurch? Because these behemoths, defined as any church having more than two thousand in attendance, seemed to be the wave of the future. They are growing twice as fast as anyone ever thought they would and have spread beyond the Bible Belt to almost every state in the country. Megachurches do religion with an excellence that nobody else can match. If I was going to report on an evangelical faith that had all the strengths I remembered, intact and magnified, megachurches were the place to do it.

Let me stop here and define what I meant by *evangelicals* when I began. I meant those people who have accepted Jesus as their personal savior and as the only way to heaven, who accept the Bible as the inerrant word of God, and who are scaring the bejesus out of the rest of America. We might even call them Rove-ite evangelicals, after George W. Bush's political adviser who used them so well that the most fervent members of the Southern Baptist Convention and other so-called Bible-based churches have come to define evangelical faith in the popular mind. They are often called the Religious Right.

Sometimes I will use that term, in lowercase, to denote the kind of uniform conservatism these evangelicals exhibit in their opinions and their lives. I will be using the term in a broad social, and only occasionally political, sense. They aren't the only evangelicals, but these days they're the only ones that count. Later my definition of *evangelicalism* would become more sophisticated than the four points I just mentioned, but those points were where I started, and they pretty much sum up what most Americans mean when they talk of evangelicals. At that time, I believed evangelical power to be enormous.

Evangelicals appeared to be racking up victories most Americans never dreamed they would. They got credit for electing their anointed one, George W. Bush, as president for the second time. They seemed to control Congress, were credited with convincing school boards to teach creationism, and had stalled movement toward granting gay rights across the country. They had worked to make abortions difficult to attain in many states, persuaded the U.S. government to cut family-planning services from international aid, and secured a Supreme Court that very well might outlaw abortion altogether. They had convinced pharmacists that supplying birth control is immoral and were trying to convince women that using it is against God's will. Their power was increasing in southern strongholds and spreading so widely that author Kevin Phillips called what was happening the southernization of American politics.

Political power was in some ways the least of it. They had split the Methodists, Presbyterians, and Episcopalians asunder and were stealing multitudes of Roman Catholics away from the mother church. Whenever issues of moral conduct were raised, reporters turned to these most conservative evangelicals as though they held the entire franchise on such matters. All over the country, it seemed as if communities and families were being divided between nonevangelicals and new superfervent evangelicals, separated by a deepening chasm that none of us knew how to bridge. Evangelical forces seemed stronger than they'd ever been, and they seemed to be growing.

Evangelicals appeared to be witnessing everywhere, talking their talk so loudly that the rest of us couldn't escape it. Restaurants, hotels, airports. On Hawaiian beaches, on New York street corners, in Colorado suburbs. In 2006 Southern Baptists, the most politically powerful evangelical group in the country and the largest Protestant denomination in the nation, launched a campaign to baptize 1 million new believers in one year. Evangelical enemies were trembling, and friends were rejoicing. They seemed to have endless power, money, people, commitment—and from all appearances they were getting more.

But as I moved behind the scenes, insiders kept cautioning me about weaknesses hidden behind the headlines. "Don't just look at the front door. Look at who's going out the back door," several church experts cautioned. "Figure out why we're not converting anyone," said a successful megachurch preacher. "I believe if Jesus were to return and rapture his people, 50 percent of the people here would show up on Sunday and say where'd everybody go?" a Baptist church staffer told me.

Then the world's most well known evangelical pollster, George Barna, wrote a book stating that the evangelical church as we know it is beginning to die. Twenty million fervent believers are getting their primary spiritual experience outside churches already, he wrote. In twenty years, only one-third of the population will look to churches primarily or exclusively for experiencing and expressing their faith.

Other data show that roughly one thousand evangelicals walk away from churches every day and most don't come back. As for those splendid megachurches, the pride of the evangelical world, they're dinosaurs and don't yet know it. I heard that last one over and over again from insiders who ought to know. Megachurches soon will be like Old West ghost towns, one former megachurch leader said. People will be taking tours of them as examples of a bygone era.

I was listening but not believing. Young people have always pulled away from church and then come back. Megachurches are popping up everywhere, richer and bigger each day. Membership in evangelical churches was the only success story in American churches. Those whispers of disaster seemed unfounded. Then the last tumbler clicked into place. The Southern Baptist Convention's 2006 effort to baptize 1 million people in one year ended, and the baptism figures came in. Not only did the Baptists fall two-thirds short of their goal; they baptized fewer people in 2006 than they had the year before. How was that possible?

No one piece of evidence was enough on its own, but as I continued to research I found one evangelical shortfall after another, and they began to form into an astonishing pattern of fact. Just as I had finished convincing myself that the evangelical church was smarter and had more to offer than ever—I'm still convinced of that—I was hit with the growing suspicion that the entire faith might be sinking fast. Then I discovered that my suspicion was backed by the evangelicals' own statistics. I might not have trusted anyone else's.

The pattern is indisputable. The whisperers are right. If Satan is waging war against the evangelicals, as many of them believe, it's beginning to look like a rout. If the kind of Christianity that has been bedrock for American values is about to go the way of the butter churn, somebody ought to be sounding an alarm. Blowing a trumpet. Singing hosannas? I don't know which, but if the rumors are true, something vital in our heritage is about to be lost.

I went back to my megachurch notes. I looked at the stories again, searching for reasons that evangelicals' strong testimonies of faith, with their tremendous rewards and assurances, might fail to compel modern Americans as they had for generations. I researched more. I soon realized what any philosopher, maybe any theologian, certainly any historian, might have told me. Their virtues are killing them as surely as their vices. To understand what's happening, you'll need to understand both.

✓*Part One*

THE DUPING OF AMERICA

One

Chpt. 1) gres to pg. 14 =

GOD IN SKIN

Evangelical faith and the numbers around it are not all puffery, and that, of course, is what makes the truth so hard to find. Underneath the hype, there is a true foundation, a real faith that still inspires, a power that all the gods of modernity can never match. Science, psychology, individualism, freedom, democracy—all are wondrous but limited. None can give divine purpose, eternal comfort, ultimate justice, enduring community. Old-time religion does. Now more than ever, in the fearful, lonely days we live in, those gifts are worth their price. Considering that Americans are a practical people, always able to know a good deal when they see it, evangelical faith should not be dying in America. And therein lies the paradox. Because it is dying. And it has been since the 1900s.

As I continued to research, a split-screen picture formed. On one side of the screen were the believers. Many of them showed dazzling lives of triumphant faith that exceeded any expectation I might have had. Then I looked on the other side of the screen. That's where the numbers were. As I studied those numbers, I began to hear the preachers' warnings with new ears. Where I had once heard exaggeration, I now heard an urgency bordering on panic. They were frightened. They knew the numbers, and they knew what they meant. It was the rest of the country that was being deceived

Before we're through, I'll show you a lot of those numbers. I'll show you that there aren't nearly as many true, rock-ribbed evangelicals in the country as we've been led to believe. I'll show you that baptisms are down and dwindling. I'll show you that devout believers are abandoning the Christian faith in droves. I'll show you that the behavior and the attitudes of the great mass of evangelicals aren't what we think they are. I'll show you that the mightiest of the evangelical churches are on the edge of a fall.

To get a complete picture of how strong evangelicals appear to be in contrast to how weak they actually are, you must toggle back and forth between those two screens. First we'll look at the stories of transforming faith; then we'll look at the numbers that belie them. Both represent a true reality. As you'll see from the stories I'm about to tell, if evangelicals really had the numbers they say they have and were growing the way people think they are, they would be unstoppable. But they don't have the numbers, and they aren't growing. The demise of evangelical faith in America is the crash of a titan, a loss of enormous proportions. Underrate it and you will also misunderstand the enormous strength of the forces that are killing it.

Who's to blame? When evangelical insiders aren't blaming Satan for the decline, they blame the churches. They can't blame God, and they can't blame the Bible. So they blame the churches. If the churches were at fault, fixing the problems would be easy. Change the churches, and people will start being saved again. But the churches aren't to blame. Modern life, changed circumstances, the new realities that we live among are to blame. The churches are doing a bang-up job delivering what evangelical faith promises. To show how good a job, I'll take you inside a

Ctpt I (cont)

Southern Baptist church in Rockwall, Texas, called Lake Pointe Church.

Lake Pointe is a ten-thousand-person organization of volunteers who give hundreds of thousands of hours and more than $12 million each year to their cause. Evangelical churches all over the country inspire similar behavior and giving. After months of research on them, my biggest question was one I had never imagined asking: "Why isn't everybody joining?" I'll warn you before we start that some ideas and behavior in these stories are going to sound so strange that many people will be tempted to reject them straightaway. Partly that's because evangelicals use spiritual language that's no longer heard in common parlance and because, like every strong group, they learn to communicate in a sort of verbal shorthand that has depths of meaning to it but sounds like jargon and nonsense to others. The truths evangelicals tell about their lives also confuse outsiders because we live in a society where many functions of religion have been taken over by psychology. This transformation has been so widespread that people outside evangelical circles have largely lost the ability to understand the truths of inner experience when they are expressed in religious language. Whenever I can, I'll translate this language into concepts that will let outsiders understand better.

We will start with Van Grubbs, the man at Lake Pointe who is in charge of giving away a quarter of a million dollars every year. I hope his story and other stories of evangelical faith I'll tell later will cause you to doubt the assertions I've made about the death of evangelical faith and influence. I hope you start to think I must be either deluded or a liar. You'll be exactly where I was every time I went back to Lake Pointe.

EACH MORNING, MAKING his way toward Lake Pointe Church, which waits for him like a green concrete dirigible grounded in the heavy fume and growl of Interstate 30, Van Grubbs passes Rockwall city hall. Each morning Van, the community-ministries director for the church, raises his hand, palm flat out, toward the car window that faces the civic building and prays, "Oh, Lord, I love you so much. Thank you for what you've done for me. Use me in a mighty way and to your glory not mine. May my mouth be yours. May my ears be yours, my arms be yours. Tell me how to use the atoms in my body for your glory." Christians are nothing but God in skin, he likes to say.

Contrast Van's morning routine with those of the drivers around him, listening to news of another day's disasters, laughing at raunchy repartee from radio's latest shock jocks, cursing the traffic, speeding to make the light, worrying, regretting, planning. Van, meanwhile, is positioning himself amid the greatest good conceivable. He's affirming that he is part of that goodness, that he is powerful and true-hearted, someone of eternal importance. As he spends the next eight hours disbursing the church's $250,000 annual benevolence budget, he and God will communicate many times. His God is all-powerful, all-knowing, and intimately connected with everything that's happening in his life. He and God have a relationship. Who wouldn't want that? Especially when that relationship helps Van in every way, particularly in doing the good work at hand.

It is easy for the needy to reach him and easy for him to respond creatively. No bureaucracy surrounds him, no barbed-wire cage of regulations. During his day he'll speak directly to the longtime poor, who know exactly what the church has to give, when it gives it, and when they're eligible to get again. About 50 percent of his visitors are these regulars, who always return on exactly the day they're eligible for another handout. He generally gives it to them. He'll entertain travelers who saw the church at the side of the road on their way across Texas and figured that a quick stop might garner easy gas money. He'll be visited by the newly unemployed who sometimes need big bucks, enough to pay the mortgage for their six-hundred-thousand-dollar lakeside homes.

Rockwall County, which sits on Lake Ray Hubbard about twenty-five miles east of Dallas, is in one of the best-educated and wealthiest counties in the nation, but the dot-com bust hit Rockwall and all of Dallas's upper-income suburbs hard. Texas Instruments and the telecommunications industry are big employers in this area of North Texas, which means the hits haven't stopped coming. Rockwall County's foreclosure rate has been going up every year for years. The church's average attendance of ten thousand comes not only from wealthy Rockwall but from cities and counties around the town that are far less prosperous.

Those who seek help from Van come through the double glass doors, up the wide staircase, and are announced by women at the front desk, who read the Bible between visitors and phone calls. Van, a thin fifty-four-year-old with brown curly hair worn long enough to halo around his head and fall in a thick pile over his collar, will rise from behind the desk in his windowless office and come forward into the hall with his hand outstretched. Petitioners sit on hard-back chairs around a little table as they plead their need. First thing Van likes to say is: "If you get anything good out of this, it's coming from God. If it's bad, I apologize. It came from me. It slipped through."

Van never goes home worrying that he made the wrong decision that day. It's in God's hands. He often cries with those who need his help, but he never lies awake at night depressed by what he's heard. One reason, he told me, is that a problem in brain wiring impedes communication with the left and right hemispheres of his brain, which keeps him from remembering much. He counts his forgetfulness as one of God's blessings, a preparation perhaps for the work God had in store for him. If he couldn't forget all the sad stories he hears each week, he wouldn't be able to do his work.

He is also at peace because he believes that his faith has transformed him completely: "It is through my faith in that I become righteous because God can't stand me as a sinner. He can't stand to be around me. In order to be around me he's got to make me righteous. So even in my sin when I am sitting here, and something comes through and it comes from me and not from God, I am still fully righteous. So I can put my head on my pillow tonight. I don't have to feel bad or guilty, because God has made me fully righteous. That's what the Bible tells me."

Pretty strong stuff. "I tell people your esteem is in Christ," Van continued. "When you're fully loved, fully forgiven, fully whole, even with Jesus, your esteem is in Christ. You're perfect. Don't let anybody tell you different—not your mother, not your dad, not your boss."

From morning to night, Van knows who he is, where he stands in the universe, and what he is to do with his life. He knows that God is always ready to help him. Van and his church also know exactly what their benevolence office is about, and it isn't charity. That's only a sideline. They are giving away money so people will feel touched by the love of God and respond to it. They consider God's love the most precious gift they have to give. Some people take that gift by accepting Jesus as their lord and master, but even in the lavish setting of a megachurch, where the great riches available to God's people are amply evident, most of them don't. It's not because Van shirks the task of offering it.

One of the first things he asks is whether a person has been saved by the grace of Jesus, wants to be, or is still thinking about whether he wants to. To supplicants who protest, Van says, "The church is not a grocery store or a gas station; it is a spiritual institution. So the first thing we're going to do is spiritual. Yes, I have a food pantry. Yes, I have some gift cards for gas. Yes, we do those things, but that's not what we are. Our mission at Lake Pointe Church is 'Share Christ, build believers.' Everything we do must have that as its purpose or we're not being true to our mission."

In the first half of the interview, as supplicants fill out a financial sheet and tell their story, Van plays good cop, and in the last half he is often bad cop.

"I repeat back what I've heard. I look at the sheet. I say, 'Here's what I feel that God is saying that you need to hear right now,' and at the end they're still wondering, 'So how much of my utility bill are you going to pay?' They're not hearing most of it."

So he draws them a picture, a diagram that demonstrates what he's saying. Sometimes he doesn't give people what they want. "Say someone comes in and they don't have a job," he said as an example. And he quoted, "'He who doesn't work, doesn't eat.' That's biblical." Some people go away mad. Some people go away and never return. And that's all right.

"If they come in here, they're going to hear what God has to say to them. If they don't want to hear it . . . ?" he asks, a rhetorical question that he answers with a dismissive shrug.

"What God has to say through you?" I ask.

"Correct."

"How do you know these messages are from God?" Van was the second Lake Pointe person I'd asked that question of and the second person to tell me that my question is one that can never be fully understood by an unbeliever. They both used the same analogy.

"When you talk about being a Christian and when you talk about faith and you talk about God speaking, it's like, go to a blind person who has never seen and try to tell him about the color violet. It can't be done," Van explained to me.

True enough. How anyone might be in a relationship with an invisible entity who never speaks audibly is a mystery to outsiders, but plenty have tried to figure out what's going on. One of them was Carl Jung. He believed that religion allowed the conscious mind to connect with the universal unconscious. He saw the unconscious as the great unknown of human experience, a repository of knowledge and wisdom that transcended individual experience. Others might reject Jung's universal unconscious and say religion connects people with their own personal unconscious and that is reward enough. Whichever explanation you accept, Van's sense that he is in touch with something more powerful than himself, something that is defined by an ancient, infallible book, allows him to offer a gift beyond reckoning— eternal safety.

"I have people come in here and say, 'Van, if I don't get five hundred thousand dollars right on up to one million dollars, I'm going to be dead in six months. I need a liver transplant.' Ummm. Oh, man. My heart goes out to them. I say, 'I have good news and I have bad news. Good news is you are going to be OK. Bad news may be that you're going to be in heaven sooner than you thought, 'cause I don't know who's got five hundred thousand dollars or a million dollars to pay for that liver transplant. That is an entitlement issue.'" Van doesn't have that much money, but he does have something else to offer:

"That gives me a great opportunity to really look at their salvation and find the peace that passes understanding. This isn't me. It's God. I get no glory. God gets all the glory, OK?"

Because Van believes he can ensure an eternal happy ending, he can make reality-based statements about the nature of life that would seem heartless in other circumstances. Sometimes you die. Sometimes you lose. Sometimes life doesn't get better. Those things are terrible but true, and Van is able to say them without being cold or uncaring or even utterly despairing because he believes that no matter what you've lost, he has something better. Eternal forgiveness; heaven; divine comfort. A higher, nobler purpose; a new identity.

Van never worries that people will conceal their finances or fudge on frivolous spending or say they are Christian when they are not, because he believes God will tell him the truth. Sometimes God tells Van to help people, and sometimes he tells Van to act prophetically, which is Van's way of saying he confronts people. God is unpredictable, and Van doesn't always agree with what he dictates. "I've had people, in all honesty, sitting out there and I know their case and I go, 'I'm not going to help them this time.' They make me mad. And God will say, 'Oh yes you are.' And I do.

"We've had people come to the Lord in this office. I've had Satan in this office twice. I actually threw my hands up and I said, 'In the name of Jesus Christ, Satan be gone.' And I slammed my hands on the table.

"How did I know they were Satan? By what I was hearing, being challenged by, what they were demanding, I don't know. God just said to me, 'Whoa, you need to do an exorcism on this person.'

"There was an aura and a presence. The people at the reception saw it, too. It wasn't mental illness. Your heart just goes out to them, but when someone comes in here with evil intent, to take you down, or to do something to affect you as a bodily person, man, I put on the armor of Christ and do battle." Both men left Van's office without violence. But Van wasn't worried.

"If someone were to come in here and kill me, I know where I'm going. So I don't care. I'm not afraid. It doesn't scare me. I just do what God tells me to do. That sounds real trite and I don't mean to sound that way. That's just how I run my life.

"Your life here is nothing but a little dot."

People who want him to show them the money and shut up would be best advised to deny intimate acquaintanceship with Jesus, and they certainly should not admit to being a member at Lake Pointe. Van, and presumably God through him, takes a special interest in making sure believers are held to the proper standards.

"I have Christians who come in here, and I say, 'I'm not going to doubt your salvation, but if he's the Lord of your life why are you in such deep crisis right now? You've been in control of your life a little bit too long.'

"I will have people come in here who I will challenge. Man was sitting there and he said, 'Van, I need six thousand dollars tomorrow or I'm going to lose my house.'

"'You're a member?'

"'Yes.'

"'You have an ABF?'" ABF is short for "adult Bible fellowship," a better-organized, more demanding megachurch version of what used to be called Sunday school and now is commonly called *small group*.

The man answered that yes, he was a member of an ABF.

"'Have you shared this problem with your ABF?'

"'No.'

"'Why? Pride. OK. Can't give what you don't have. Can't accept what you don't have room for. You're not going to see God's love until you get rid of pride, till you get rid of some junk in your life and make room for what is good.'

"'I have good news and bad news. The bad news is you've lost a job making six hundred thousand dollars a year. You're going to lose your house tomorrow. That's reality.'

"We cried together. I do a lot of crying in here. Good news is God is going to give you what you need. Not what you want, not your entitlements, not your lifestyle—what you need."

What happened next to the man who was about to lose his house still brings tears to Van's eyes. "He shared it with his ABF. Three families went over to his house, with their children, while they're packing, and said, 'You know what? Your kids need a party. This has got to be stressful. We're going to have a party for your kids. Here's fifty dollars and tickets to the AMC movie theater. You need a date. We are so concerned about your marriage. You're about to lose your home.'

"Man!" Van says, pumping his fist in a victory salute. "It's the body of Christ putting on skin and helping each other and people outside the body of Christ.

"End of story, the man now makes forty-two thousand dollars working at the airport. They have a little house in Garland. He sat here and I said, 'The four walls you live in is about to change and what you drive is about to change because you're here with a lifestyle issue.'"

I ought to add, in closing this chapter, that Van Grubbs was once a minister in a more liberal Christian tradition. His faith was transformed while attending Lake Pointe. He has experienced many of the tragedies he hears about in his job. He lost his livelihood several times; his first wife divorced him for another person. His health is precarious, and he is in constant pain. And yet he lives a life of perfect security. He can accept change with equanimity and counter tragedy with hope. He has the authority to tell others the kind of hard truths that might help them do the same, and sometimes they follow his advice. Faced with dangerous men, he calls on the Lord and feels delivered. Confronting the idea of death, he feels a sense of ease. He is able to do those things because he worships a time-honored version of God—a big, powerful, sometimes vengeful, sometime merciful, and yet always intimately connected God. He loves that God, and he fears him. They have a relationship.

Let's for a minute put aside all the controversial otherworldly promises that Van's religion makes. Forget heaven and hell. Disregard promises of eternal life. Ignore the idea that God talks to Van. Just look at the quality of Van's days compared with the insecurity, uncertainty, and sheer tedious, mundane nature of the lives many of us lead, and maybe you too will wonder why everybody isn't an evangelical.

But everybody isn't. In fact, only a small minority of Americans are the Van Grubbs kind of evangelical, a much smaller minority than we have been led to believe. Van believes that's true even at his church. He is the minister who told me that if the rapture came today, half the people at Lake Pointe would show up Sunday wondering where everyone went. He isn't the only person who said such things. Almost every Lake Pointe member I talked to said something similar.

cht.
Two ⟩ goes to p. 32

ONE OUT OF FOUR AMERICANS?

The most popular statistic we hear about evangelicals is that they make up 25 percent of America. That would be 54 million adult evangelicals; add kids and you're up to 75 million people. If one out of four Americans is a version of Van Grubbs, the rest of the country can give it up. They're invincible. They know who they are, they know what they want, and they believe wholeheartedly that God is with them. But even insiders like Van and others in the Lake Pointe congregation don't think all those people are true evangelicals in the fully committed, fully conservative, fully biblical way that they are.

The idea that 25 percent of Americans are evangelicals of that kind began to be widely broadcast after the 2000 presidential election when evangelicals were credited with giving George W. Bush the election. Their reputation was solidified in 2004 when the so-called value voters, also about 25 percent, were cast as evangelicals with a hard-right agenda. Who were these value voters/evangelicals? According to the first stories that were published, always the ones that people remember, they were those who wanted abortion banned. They wanted schools to teach creationism, celebrate Christmas, ban Halloween, cast out unsuitable books, and hold public prayers. They opposed all gay rights. They supported the Iraq war and approved of any means necessary to get information from prisoners. They favored business, opposed taxes, and believed that separation of church and state should be abolished.

After the initial value-voters reports were published, journalists and scholars began to challenge whether these voters actually were who they were said to be. They pointed out that to many people "values" might mean and in fact *did* mean something very different from what was being assumed, but by then the notion that a huge number of Americans, capable of delivering presidential elections, held monolithic, evangelical views was set. And so the two numbers came together. One out of four Americans came to be seen as churchgoing, fervent evangelicals of rigid and uniform opinions who voted to support hard-right political positions for religious/value reasons.

But was that true? To figure out if there truly are 54 million evangelicals, the best way to start is by asking how that figure was obtained. It comes two ways: from asking people what their religious affiliation is, and from statistics put out by the churches. That seems solid enough until you realize that neither of these sources has the slightest impartiality. First let's take the individual responses. Everyone knows that certain questions— How often do you have sex? Do you take drugs? Do you go to church?—are answered truthfully so rarely that there's hardly any reason to bother asking. The only valid information they give comes from year-to-year comparisons, and those comparisons tell us only whether what Americans say is changing or not changing. Are more people calling themselves evangelicals this year than last? Are fewer people saying they're Baptist this year than last year? They tell us how what people say about themselves is changing, and that tells us something about how society as a whole is changing. It doesn't tell us much, because we don't know what the changes mean or what is causing them. And, more important, such statistics reveal almost nothing about what Americans actually do. That's because while some people are reflecting their behavior perfectly, others are telling more subjective truths—and nobody knows which people are doing what.

Let me give you some commonly quoted religion statistics that illustrate my point. Eighty percent of Americans say they are Christians, but everybody knows that true Christianity isn't something measured with one question, and everyone also knows that "I'm a Christian" is the easy answer, the culturally safe answer, the one many of us would give ourselves just to get off the hook. Sixty-two percent of Americans tell pollsters they are church members. Better surveys ask if people have gone to church in the past week, and they find that 40 percent of Americans say yes. That seems closer to what experience and observation tell us, but the figure is also somewhat alarming. If only 40 percent even say they have gone in the last week, how many really did? Half that?

When researchers Kirk Hadaway and Penny Marler went to. churches and counted, that is exactly what they found. Only 20 percent of Americans actually were in church. Were those other 20 percent lying? Not exactly. They were reflecting that they grew up going to church, or that they meant to go to church, or that they supported going to church even though they didn't go themselves—or that although they weren't in church last Sunday, they usually were in church or thought they were or wanted to be and so saying they weren't would give the wrong impression. Saying that they went to church wasn't the literal truth, wrote Hadaway. It was the subjective truth. For more than half of the people it was what they believed about themselves or wanted others to believe, or it was merely a measure of their aspirations.

And sometimes it's not even that much. Sometimes people just want to let the pollster know that they are on the side of God and the good people.[1]

So what we have here is that 80 percent of people say they are Christians, 40 percent say they went to church in the last week, and 20 percent—one-fourth of those who claimed to be Christians, actually were there. Could something similar be true of evangelicals? If 25 percent say they're evangelicals, could it be that one-fourth of that number, 6 percent, actually are church-going evangelicals? That's too shaky an inference. It yields too extreme a number. To accept such a number would take much more evidence.

So let's look at the other way that religion statistics are gathered, which is by accepting what the churches say about themselves. Churches aren't any better sources than individuals, not only because they also have a reason to misrepresent, but because of the way they keep records. This is true of all the churches, not just the evangelical ones. In the Roman Catholic Church, for instance, a baby who is baptized Catholic is a Catholic all her life. She may leave and join a Methodist church and a few years later join a Baptist church and then perhaps become a Pentecostal at an independent church. She may then drop out and never go back to church. But she's still on the rolls. She might be counted as being a member of four churches even though she no longer attends any of them.

Or a person who is heavily invested in religion may join or attend several churches on a regular basis. Scott Thumma, one of the country's most prominent researchers, says this practice seems to be increasing. In his research on megachurches, it is common to find the most committed Christians engaged enough in multiple churches that they might be counted on all the church rolls. They might join several churches at once, he said. When I appeared shocked at that idea, which would have seemed traitorous in the small towns where I grew up, he laughed and said, "What's wrong with that?" As more and more churches have begun to count members as those who attend rather than those who actually sign up as members, the double, triple, and even quadruple counting of Christians has only gotten more pervasive. The anonymity of megachurches also contributes by allowing Christians who have burned out working too hard in smaller churches to keep their membership in a home church while they begin attending a megachurch that will let them rest up. They would easily be counted on both rolls.

Since all churches have similar accounting challenges, church statistics aren't much good if all you do is quote the big numbers. But if you look underneath to what researchers inside the church are saying to their pastors, you can get a clearer picture. A good place to do that is with the biggest evangelical group in the country: the Southern Baptist Convention.

Except for Catholics, who are the largest religious group in America, Southern Baptists dwarf everybody else—in organization, money, people, and record-keeping. If Southern Baptists, who are also by far the biggest Protestant denomination and almost six times bigger than the next-biggest white evangelical denomination in the country, aren't as numerous as they say they are, evangelicals take a big hit.[2] The Southern Baptist Convention says it has more than 16 million members. But how many of those members go to church? How often do they go? How much do they participate in church activities? Do they believe the basic doctrines of the Southern Baptist Convention? Does their behavior reflect those beliefs and doctrines? Those are the questions we need to answer in order to know how many true, Bible-believing, religious-right evangelicals there are in the nation's largest Protestant denomination. When we know that, we'll have a start to knowing whether the bulk of those who are being considered religious-right evangelicals are actually who we think they are.

But those answers aren't easy to find. Let's start with the simplest question. How many of those 16 million Southern Baptists actually go to church?

"The reality is, the FBI couldn't find half of those [16 million members] if they had to," the Reverend Thomas Ascol of Grace Baptist Church in Cape Coral, Florida, told Religion News Service reporter Amy Green. He's probably right, but Ascol is seen by many within the denomination as a spoiler. He's a Calvinist, a man who believes that no one can be saved unless his name is in God's book of life, and no one knows whose name is or isn't in the book. The rise of this type of Calvinist in the Southern Baptist Convention is a relatively new development, and lots of people are alarmed by it. One reason is that Calvinists like Ascol would like to get all the slackers, whom he and other Calvinists call the unregenerate, out of the church. He has submitted resolutions at the Southern Baptist Convention to clean up the rolls, and has been turned down.

So how could we know whether he was right or wrong?

Several Southern Baptists directed me to look at the annual reports of the Southern Baptist Convention. Sure enough, those reports gave Ascol some support. The 2006 report showed that out of 16.3 million members only 11 million, or about two-thirds, are even residents of the same town as the churches they belong to.

These aren't necessarily devoted members, mind you, but at least they live close enough to church that they wouldn't need an airline ticket to get there. The 11 million figure includes those who've joined more than one Baptist church and are being double counted. Baptists try to avoid double counting by notifying churches about membership changes, but it doesn't always work, partly because people who have been out of church for a while may not tell their new church that they're still on another church's rolls. They may not know it. The 11 million includes all those people who are still in town but go to church only on Easter and Christmas or not even that often. It includes people who've joined churches of other faiths and never let the Baptists know. It includes people who aren't coming to church and don't intend to ever come to church. Since nobody takes roll at the church door, it's hard to know who is or who isn't coming to church, especially in a big church.

How many members a church has is a pretty worthless measure of reality. Even asking how many attend church services doesn't mean a whole lot if we're talking about true commitment, but at least that number is an estimate of those actually present. The SBC 2007 annual report shows 6,138,776 in attendance at primary worship services. That number is backed up by other studies through the years that consistently show attendance to be much lower than membership figures. Attendance figures get us closer but they also have some problems with double counting since many people attend multiple churches throughout the year. Southern Baptist researchers themselves note that many of those who attend aren't members and that one out of eight of them isn't even saved. If we factor out that one in eight who is unsaved, the number of people in Southern Baptist churches on an average Sunday, 5.3 million, is getting close now to the kind of committed evangelicals we think of when we think about evangelicals who are having so much effect on the country. But people who merely come to main church services still aren't those any insider would call the faithful. They may or may not give money and time to the church. They may or may not think about the sermon or read their Bibles or pray or agree with the preacher on most points of Scripture. They may be there for free babysitting in the church nursery, for the music, for sociability.

In assessing the true health of any church, only one number really counts, only one question gets it: "'Bout how many do you run in Sunday school?" People in Sunday school aren't all true followers, but they're about as close as numbers can get you. The majority of them give money, they give time, they pray, they read their Bibles. They are a pretty good measure of the people we're talking about when we talk about evangelicals who are committed to the same principles as the religious right. Southern Baptists consider enrollment and attendance at Sunday school to be only the second step in making disciples of Christians. Daily prayer, daily Bible reading, accountability to other Christians for one's behavior, tithing, as well as service to the church and the public are all better hallmarks of the devoted evangelical who fits the public's perception of a religious right evangelical, but those matters are almost impossible to measure. Even if surveys are available, they have the same problem that polls of church attendance do. People's perception and accounts of their behavior often don't match their actual behavior.

The definition of Sunday school has enlarged in recent years as churches have begun to expand classes beyond Sunday and rename them Bible studies, or Bible fellowships or small groups. These groups may or may not meet at church. They may meet any day of the week and at any time. They are often more rigorously organized than traditional Sunday schools. The church growth movement that has produced so many megachurches has typically re-cast these small groups as small churches with strong leaders. At churches such as Lake Pointe, small groups are vital in the growth of the church and have many layers of commitment and numerous goals. We'll discuss these groups in greater detail later.

So how many Southern Baptists are in these Sunday schools or their equivalent on a given week? Despite all the innovation and flexibility now in place, Sunday school attendance as a percentage of worship service attendance has declined precipitously since 1991, when worship service attendance first began to be reported. In 1991, it was 85.5 percent. In 2005, the percentage was 68.5 percent, according to the SBC 2007 annual report. Southern Baptist churches now maintain an average Sunday school enrollment of 8.1 million members with average attendance of about half that, 4.1 million, according to Southern Baptist records.

I could hardly believe these numbers even though they were produced by the Baptists themselves. The 2007 annual report noted that churches are beginning to realize that classes held on days other than Sunday should be counted as Sunday school. That seemed to mean that there might now be confusion over what Sunday school really is. But then, when I looked at an internal report on attendance figures from 1997, I found almost the same ratios. So the figures were solid and not being distorted by vocabulary. I still couldn't believe it. These were averages. I argued against accepting them by reasoning that maybe Southern Baptists were doing other things on a lot of Sundays and the crowd was turning over so much that averages didn't represent as much as they should. Then I found another measure, in the 2006 Southern Baptist annual report. The Women's Missionary Union (WMU) is perhaps the most powerful organization in Southern Baptist life. They work hard, they raise money, and, when they want to, they can pretty much tell a church how to behave. I looked at the enrollment of the WMU and of the men and boys enrollment in equivalent organizations. They totaled about 1.2 million people. That would mean that one out of four people in attendance at Sunday school belonged to the main missionary groups in a denomination that is fervently devoted to missionary activity. That sounded about right. Still, those groups were a big commitment. There's been controversy around the WMU, often because it won't cede as much power to the male leaders as the men want. Once again I argued that perhaps those figures weren't telling enough.

Then I found another measure that again supported the same conclusion.

Every year the Southern Baptists ask for money for a special fund, the Annie Armstrong offering for North American missions. This donation is one of the two most important offerings of the Southern Baptist year. It is relentlessly promoted and tremendously important to Baptists. This one came from the 2007 annual report, which shows that Southern Baptists gave only $57 million to that offering, and officials were delighted with that amount. It was $2 million more than their goal. But measure it out. If Southern Baptists have 16 million members, then each of them gave a bit over $3.50 to the most important North American missions offering of the year. If they have 8 million members, each of them gave a little over $7. Only if they have 4 million people contributing do they begin to approach a reasonable amount of money, a little over $14 apiece, for Southern Baptists who are and always have been aggressively mission-minded people.

Under 4 million is in fact the correct number of true, devoted, church-loving, right-thinking, probably-are-religious-right-voting Southern Baptists in this country according to the Baptists' own count. Some of those are being double, triple, or even quadruple counted because they go to several Sunday schools or their equivalent adult Bible fellowships. Among them are a fair number of Democrats and closet moderates just keeping quiet about it. I could show you numbers on that, too. But never mind. Around 4 million people are in Sunday school, and about a million more are in attendance at church services on Sunday according to the Southern Baptists themselves.

Now let's think about the other evangelicals. Southern Baptists are the best-organized group in the evangelical world—by far. Southern Baptists are record-keeping fiends with a strong, well-financed core organization. Most other evangelicals belong to small denominations or Bible churches that are independent or affiliated with small groups of like-minded churches. Only one national group, the National Association of Evangelicals, has brought these evangelicals together. The NAE lists sixty-one of these denominations, including Pentecostals and charismatics of various kinds, as members and has claimed that they represent 30 million evangelicals. Because of that claim, NAE leaders are prominent spokesmen for evangelicals. (Southern Baptists are not among the groups, so we aren't double counting in that way, although those churches certainly have double counted many members.)

I looked for each of those sixty-one denominations in the three best national resources for church membership statistics— the U.S. Congregational Survey, the *Yearbook of American and Canadian Churches 2007,* and the American Religion Statistical Archives—and on the denominations' own Web sites. I found all but ten of them. The total number of their adherents? 7.6 million. The other ten groups aren't even prominent enough to be mentioned in American religion archives. Some of the groups appear to be evangelistic organizations or service groups that help the church, not actual denominations. I e-mailed the ones I could find.

I called the National Association of Evangelicals' director of member services and asked him where the 30 million membership figure came from. He said the "vast majority are in the denominations" listed on the Web site, and the association uses the numbers supplied to them by the denominations. The research archives I used also got their numbers from the denominations and churches. So 7.6 million, which is a fourth of the 30 million the association is thought to have, would seem to be about right.

When I first looked at the National Association of Evangelicals Web site in the spring of 2007, the sixty-one churches and denominations were called the association's anchor. Where were the other 22.4 million members? The NAE Web site said the association's constituency includes tens of millions of individuals and organizations. That might be true, just as my constituency might be every reader who has ever read my books or newspaper articles or listened to a radio interview I've done or e-mailed me or attended one of my lectures or stopped by when I was promoting books in a bookstore. They could number in the millions, tens of millions. But if I were to say that I speak for 23 million people and present myself as someone who leads them, I would be overstepping my authority quite egregiously. However, if I could get the news media and politicians to accept my contention, I would become quite powerful. Image is everything.

When I called NAE president Leith Anderson in August 2007 for a final comment, he said the 30 million figure should not be on the Web site, and most references to it do appear to be gone now. He usually says the NAE represents millions of evangelicals or forty-five thousand churches. The organization's last official count, judging from the Web site, was in 1990. It showed 4.5 million members. Where did the 30 million figure come from? No one seems to know.

Now let's apply what we learned with the Southern Baptists to those 7.6 million members that the NAE has. What we learned is that the members who really count and are likely to be in church every Sunday are also in Sunday school. I took out all those denominations that I couldn't find Sunday school figures for because some denominations don't have anything like an adult Sunday school. That left me with 6.6 million members. Half of those members, 3.3 million, are members of a Sunday school or an equivalent. If we extrapolate from that, believing that Sunday school is the best measure available, that means that the actual number of committed evangelicals in the National Association of Evangelicals isn't the 30 million often claimed or the 7.6 I found on church rolls, but half the 7.6 million, or 3.8 million, about one-eighth what we've been led to believe.[3]

Judging by the Southern Baptists, that is probably half again too high. The average number of Southern Baptists enrolled in Sunday school is 8 million, as of 2007 figures. And, as we've seen, the number attending was about 4 million, one-fourth the total church membership. So one-fourth the total members in the NAE's churches, or 1.9 million, is likely to be the true number of committed, religious-right evangelicals in the NAE. But 1.9 million is such a pitiful number that once again, as with the Southern Baptists, I don't want to believe it. If we go with the 3.8 million as committed members, we will have overesti-

Clpt. 2 (cont)

27.

mated the numbers, but erring on that side means we've made up for any Southern Baptists we left out.

So now we have the two biggest evangelical organizations in the country and we have three sets of figures. If we use the numbers provided to reporters by the Southern Baptists, 16 million, and by the National Association of Evangelicals, 30 million, that would be 47 million members. Add the other evangelicals who aren't part of those groups, and it's looking pretty close to the 54 million adult members needed for evangelicals to be 25 percent of the adult population. One out of four Americans. That would mean that polls in which 25 percent of Americans claim to be evangelicals are backed up by membership statistics.

But according to membership figures from churches that belong to the National Association of Evangelicals, the NAE has about one-fourth the 30 million members it has claimed, or 7.6 million. Put those together with all 16 million Southern Baptists and you have 23.6 million evangelicals, less than half what the religious-identification polls indicate they ought to have. So now we're down to about one evangelical to every ten adult Americans. The trouble with that number is that we're using membership statistics that the churches themselves admit are tremendously inflated. These numbers are so inflated that no one within those churches would use them for planning.

When we look at the best numbers, the ones church planners really count on, Sunday school or small-group attendance, we find 4 million Southern Baptists and 3.8 million NAE evangelicals enrolled (and perhaps half that attending). We round up to 8 million. That's 8 million instead of 54 million. Not 25 percent but 3.7 percent. At last we have a number that means something. Four out of one hundred Americans are dedicated enough evangelicals to attend Sunday schools. Remember, these aren't my numbers. They're numbers published by evangelical churches themselves.

Even so, I'm not going to use that figure. It's too drastic. Let's increase that number to 5 percent and make it five out of a hundred, so as to account for any stragglers and say that committed members of the two biggest evangelical groups in the country make up 5 percent of Americans. That would not be all the evangelicals in the country. Individual Bible churches that aren't affiliated with either of these groups wouldn't be counted in that total. Many megachurches, those with more than two thousand members, are Bible churches. They are a tiny percentage of the total number of churches, but they account for a large number of members. So they might be significant. Since no one knows how many evangelicals are in those churches, let's once again be more than generous with our numbers. Let's say that 2 percent of the adult population is in an independent evangelical church that is not a part of the National Association of Evangelicals. That would be 4 million people, a generous assessment, and to be more than fair, we'll pretend that all of them attend church in a given week and go to Sunday school or a small-group equivalent. Put everything together, having given evangelicals the highest number we can using their own estimates, and we can say that conservative, churchgoing, fervent evangelicals, like those who so often dominate the news and the country's political scene, are 7 percent of the American population, not 25 percent. Remember that number, 7 percent, because we're going to encounter it again from the leading evangelical pollster in the country.

Before we do that, let's consider two reasonable questions: If this type of evangelical is so small a proportion of the population, how and why do evangelicals of this type carry such weight in national affairs? And why do 25 percent of Americans tell pollsters that they are evangelicals?

Let's take politics first. Seven percent of adult Americans is 15 million adults. That is about the number of people who live within the city limits of the country's three largest cities: New York City, Los Angeles, and Chicago. If New York, Los Angeles, and Chicago had an extremely efficient public-relations machine working constantly and brilliantly to manipulate a media that rarely questioned their statements, and their citizens had an extremely unified worldview, the sense that they were being led by God, and they all attended plenty of occasions during which their opinions could and would be shaped and they hardly ever listened to anyone outside their cities, New York, Los Angeles, and Chicago might easily control the country.

With regard to national politics, 15 million evangelical voters are even more powerful than the country's three biggest cities because evangelicals are dispersed and show up in local, state, and national elections. In the presidential elections, they are scattered enough to swing the popular and the electoral vote. In a country as evenly divided between Republicans and Democrats as this one is, any candidate who wins the popular vote by 8 percent will call it a landslide and not be contradicted. With regard to electoral politics, the great majority of evangelicals live in the South and Midwest, and are often controlled by a well-organized evangelical vote.

Politics are only part of their influence. Their opinions are solicited by reporters across the country whenever any subject they've weighed in on is broached. For instance, anywhere in the country when a story on homosexuality is written or broadcast that might seem to legitimize gay causes, it is this conservative group that is called upon for balance, rarely any of the more moderate religious leaders. The same is true of abortion rights stories.

Now let's look at the second question: Why would 25 percent of Americans say they are evangelicals if only 7 percent actually are? To answer that, we have to look at three groups that might be included in what the rest of us have been led to believe is an indivisible monolithic group. First, anybody who was ever saved in an evangelical church, or whose mother ever took them to an evangelical church, or whose community is full of evangelicals might claim that title and feel good about it. Evangelicals support patriotism, capitalism, military strength, and the idea that

America is God's special nation with the right and obligation to spread democracy. This close connection with what many consider to be American values makes it the closest thing to a civic religion that the United States has. People with little real interest in evangelical doctrine may ally themselves with all the civic values of evangelicals and happily count themselves among them.[4]

There's also a second group. The title *evangelical* is a mantle of righteousness for a lot of attitudes that don't in themselves confer much goodness. Far-right Republicans, libertarians, right-wing cranks, homophobes, racists, anti-tax crusaders, and small-government fanatics might all like counting themselves among evangelicals, who have far more clout than they do. As the evangelical-supported Institute on Religion and Democracy said in a recent article trying to pin down exactly what an evangelical is: "In the end, evangelicalism seems to be more a matter of attitude. Anyone who wants the label 'evangelical' can claim it." So what is that attitude? The sense that you're on the side of the angels and the boldness to claim it? Partly. But it is also more than that. It's a set of beliefs that come from orthodox understandings of Christianity and from Scripture. Those sources and the institutional churches that teach them give such beliefs a legitimacy that cranks, homophobes, racists, and fanatics don't have on their own—and that evangelicals themselves would never willingly give them. Politicians might. The third group is one we're going to deal with at some length later. They are born-again Christians, and many of them are members and perhaps even fairly regular attendees of evangelical churches. But their opinions and their behavior aren't anything like we've been led to expect of Bible-based evangelicals.

So is evangelical power real? Yes and no. In our times, image is everything. Historian Daniel Boorstin was perhaps the first social critic to forecast how important contrivances were becoming in American life when he wrote *The Image: A Guide to Pseudo-*

Events in America in 1961. He noted that arranged events and simulated reality were becoming so pervasive that people would say of a beautiful view, "That looks just like a postcard." He feared that such fakery on the political and social scene would cause Americans to lose touch with their true values. His observation applies to the societal power of the religious right in several ways. In this case, statistics are the postcard that is more compelling than reality. So many statistics have indicated that one out of four Americans is an evangelical that we have all come to believe it without ever contrasting what we're being told with what we see in our own lives. Deep within the Bible Belt it might be possible to find one out of four people who subscribe to strict evangelical doctrines and support ultraconservative evangelical ideas, but in the rest of the country it would be unlikely unless you belonged to an evangelical church yourself. Without ever questioning how the statistics were gathered, we believed the "image" completely. Even reporters didn't question the numbers hard enough, which meant that anyone who might profit from that image could run with it and no one would stop them.

The idea that evangelicals are one out of every four Americans adds to their legitimacy. And legitimacy is power. One voice out of four has a lot of sway. One voice out of fourteen, not so much. Reporters and politicians pay attention to groups with large numbers, and as they do, reality becomes even more distorted. The grossly inflated number of evangelicals causes us and the world to view Americans as much more religiously conservative than we are. Deflating the number of evangelicals to its true size debunks one of our most powerful national myths. It shows that the unstoppable evangelical juggernaut that has been so highly touted, revered, and feared on issue after issue is a lot of noise, a lot of smoke, and only a little bit of bang. It takes away the legitimacy that has allowed the ultraconservative evangelicals to set the country's moral agenda even though most of the country disagrees with them about what is and isn't important.

I am not saying that they have no influence at all. Fifteen million people are a lot of people, and since evangelicals are the only Protestant Christians growing in numbers, they could be on their way to making the illusion of big numbers into reality. But they aren't. We've punctured the myth of big numbers. Now let's look at growth. To do that, we'll single out the most important moment in an evangelical's life, conversion.

End of chpt. 2

Cht.   *goes to pg. 48*
Three

BECOMING HEAVEN'S BELOVED

Conversion is the moment that turns people from hell-bound to heaven's favored. It's the linchpin for all that follows. My own salvation had been a profound moment of pledging myself to seek God and to sin no more, but at the age of nine I couldn't have had much to repent of, which made my fervor small stuff compared with that of adult converts. I was in awe and a little afraid of these new believers. They burst onto the church scene explosively, on fire for God, afraid of nothing, filled with zeal. I knew when I began this project that I wanted to find someone who was newly saved. Luck was with me. I met the Tauzins my first weekend in Rockwall. I've said that to understand the fall of evangelical faith, you must understand its virtues as well as its vices. The Tauzin family's story and the story of the church that transformed their darkest hour into transcendence are decidedly on the virtue side. Perhaps only a church such as Lake Pointe, with the kind of faith it preaches, could pull off such a turn-around. But its strengths are also its weaknesses. Within the church and within the faith it preaches, all the elements crippling the evangelical nation reside side by side with all that makes the church and the faith great.

New Orleans refugees Mike and Michelle Tauzin sobbed with joy when a Southern Baptist minister brought them to Jesus in a room of the Rockwall, Texas, Holiday Inn. Even months later, when I met them, Mike could hardly recount his conversion without choking up. Michelle could not stop talking about it.

A willowy thirty-six-year-old with creamy skin and dark blond hair that curls softly down her back, Michelle was halfway through her order at Wendy's when she began to tell the food server how she and her family, flooded out by Katrina, came to Texas, to the Holiday Inn in a suburb of Dallas where people from Lake Pointe Church were looking for New Orleans refugees to help. A pastor asked if she and Mike knew Jesus, and they realized that they did not, not really, despite being Catholic all their lives. The pastor said they could give all their problems to God, and they prayed and made Jesus the lord and master of their lives. The pastor sent out for a brand-new Bible, and they wrote the date and their names in the Bible, and now they have a new Christian birthday, and later they joined Lake Pointe Church, and now . . .

Mike was looming behind her as she talked. He's a gentle man who doesn't say much. Michelle usually does the talking, in a lilting voice that moves quickly from one story to another. People sometimes stiffen as she tells about her faith; some take a step away, stop meeting her eyes, and won't reply with anything more than a grunt. Certain of her old friends have turned cool. And still the talk pours out of her, an unstoppable gush of gratitude and amazement, even though she can clearly see that the joy is all her own. And here she was, doing it again, until Mike broke in.

"Baby," Mike said in his easy Cajun way. "Baby, the lady just wants to know if you want fries with that order."

Wise words. Fries or no fries, make up your mind, make it snappy. That's how it is in the world. Tragedy could fall on any of us at any minute. The world might listen, might help, but probably not, certainly not for long. It will tire of our troubles quite quickly. We would be lucky indeed if a Southern Baptist congregation like the ten-thousand-person Lake Pointe Church reached out to help us, luckier still if we were able, as the Tauzins have, to take the best gift Lake Pointe has to offer. They joined the church not long after their conversion—another good idea—and were baptized.

Before salvation, the Tauzins had to figure out what was right and wrong every day, mostly by using their own reasoning and values. There wasn't much help. They sometimes despaired of protecting their eight-year-old son, Justin, from bad language, sex, drugs, smoking, drinking, and all the other dangers around them. They wondered whether they were being the kind of people God meant them to be. They felt alone sometimes and didn't know where to turn for advice or help. They wondered sometimes whether life had anything more to offer than just living day to day.

Now everything is different. Answers are evident; life's purpose is clear. God is always at the ready and willing to help. They are part of something bigger, wiser, better than themselves. They will never be alone again. They are born again, saved, chosen, redeemed, innocent, wiped clean of all sin, made righteous by Jesus's blood, or simply Christians, which in the United States is increasingly coming to mean only the most conservative evangelicals.

At their conversion, they had no idea how much better life was about to get. This young family was about to be gathered in by a community that would anchor their lives in a way it never had been before. The community would also name, affirm, and channel the feelings of hope and transformation that the Tauzins felt that day at the Holiday Inn. If the Tauzins were like many other evangelicals, they would soon look on the outside world as a foreign, somewhat menacing place, not nearly as good as the

Christian family they had joined. They would now see themselves as being *in* the world but not *of* the world, just as the Bible instructed.

The church would help them see the Bible as the direct word of God, an infallible, inerrant source of wisdom, a guidebook for life. They would learn to consult God's Word before making any major decision. God would speak to them through that book, guiding them toward a higher, better purpose. They would never again have to ask, "Who will help me?" or "How can I know what to do?" They would never again have to ask whether life had meaning or purpose. The answers would all be in the book; through it God would reveal truths to them that outsiders could never discern.

Although the American conservative evangelical interpretation at Lake Pointe Church is one among thousands that have been put forth since the Bible was written, Lake Pointe Church ministers call their interpretation the truth, sometimes the simple truth, and often they call it God's truth. I don't know whether it is the truth or not. I do know that calling it the truth is a good idea if you want to build a strong, motivated group. I know that accepting it as truth is better for many people than tying themselves up in the knots that constantly asking "What's the truth?" puts them into. I know it lets people get on with the business of living a good life, as the Tauzins are doing. I know that if you ever accept it as truth, you will move to a place of security that nothing else on earth can offer. I know all these things because I've been where the Tauzins now are.

Lake Pointe Church's version of biblical truth will begin to shape the Tauzins' marriage, their parenting, their finances, and their relationships with everyone and everything. The church will surround them with friends to stand with them in times of good fortune and bad. If Michelle has a baby or if illness comes to any member of the family, these new friends will organize themselves to bring meals and provide care for weeks, maybe for months. If the Tauzins are in need of money, they may go to these friends for aid, and God himself may direct the friends to help.

As the biggest and coolest church in a Bible Belt town—Lake Pointe's ten thousand average attendance makes it a third the city of Rockwall's total population—the church will give their son status at school, sports teams to join, parties to attend, and someday the chance to serve the less fortunate in countries far away. It will teach him Bible stories, help him memorize Bible verses, and as a counter to the sexual, misogynist violence of rock music, it will teach him love songs to Jesus. These songs will have a rock beat, not only holy but cool—a concept evangelical churches such as Lake Pointe understand well. Church youth ministers are often young guys with hip haircuts and easy use of the latest jargon. The Tauzins will now have guidance about which movies their son ought not to see, which books he ought not to read, and even which television programs are and are not suitable. If he accepts Christ into his own life and becomes devout, which is quite likely, the church will foster his development into a preacher, a missionary, or a stalwart man of God and caring husband. The church's upper-middle-class membership could also help Justin get into good colleges and prosper in business.

If by some unlucky circumstance he goes the other way and becomes less than totally upright, the church probably would not turn him out, certainly not if he is circumspect. In fact, it has programs that welcome just that kind of kid. Kids from all over the community use the church's skate park, its pool tables, its basketball courts. Lake Ponte is so good at drawing in sinner teens that some of them use the church's parking lots and weekly gatherings for their drug deals. Without the church's knowledge, of course. If the Tauzins ever begin to fear that their son is more interested in boys than girls—which is unlikely, of course, since he would have heard how sinful homosexuality is since childhood and would be sure to hide any such inclination if he had it—they will have lots of help in trying to turn him toward a different direction.

If the Tauzins diet, God and the church will help them. If they budget, God and the church will help them. If they sing, act, or make art, God and the church will give them a place to do it. If they become depressed, the church's therapists will counsel them. If they are without jobs, God and church will help them find work. If they are without a car or unable to fix a problem with their own cars, the church could help with that.

The Tauzins will also now be among the good people of the world. Not just in their own minds but with the imprimatur of an influential organization, one with a big building, a big parking lot, a big budget, and a big crowd. Everywhere they go in Rockwall, saying they are members of Lake Pointe will speak loudly for them. The church will help them be good, help cover for them if they fail to be good, and give them a path back to sanctity if they fail and repent.

Lake Pointe will also encourage the Tauzins to do good by pinpointing specific talents God has given them. It will give them outlets for emotions and fears that must be hidden in the outside world. Men can cry there without being thought weak. Woman can rejoice without being thought boastful. The Tauzins can confess their failings and be thought righteous for it, confess their fears and be considered strong. Their triumphs will become gifts from God; their defeats, lessons from God. Now someone will always be listening to what they say, caring about how they feel, either brothers and sisters in Christ or Christ himself.

Even if the Tauzins someday repudiate their new faith, they've encountered an aspect of human experience that's unforgettable. They are changed. Some of the changes in the Tauzins' life are internal and difficult to explain, but others are concrete. Michelle, who takes medication for depression, was once ashamed of her illness. Even Mike would hardly mention it. If she seemed to be having trouble with her mood, he might ask in a lowered tone about her "pills." Now she's willing for anyone to know. She talks about abuse in her childhood. She tells about problems in her family. None of those things, which once would have shamed her, now do. She's been made perfect in Christ, the preachers would say. *Has she really?* you might be wondering, balking understandably at such religious jargon. I don't know. But she thinks so, and so do the people of Lake Pointe. It's biblical. And if you think it, isn't it true?

Two months after they accepted the gift of salvation, I was following a rented van as the Tauzins made their way back through New Orleans toward what was left of their home. I'd invited myself along because Steve Stroope, senior pastor at Lake Pointe, was taking the family back to film a video featuring their testimony. Testimonies are the beating heart of evangelical faith, full of wonder and hope in the minds of believers, full of foolish self-delusion in the minds of scoffers. Lake Pointe testimonies, filmed, edited, and shown on the big screens at the front of the church, might include how bad a sinner you were before Jesus changed you or some wrenching misfortune that befell you and what a difference Jesus has made.

These stories bolster believers with evidence of God's work, and sometimes they can so wow unbelievers that they'll come to the Lord. They are as important for the teller as they are for the listener because they transform life from a series of events, which is what it might seem to be to a strict rationalist, into a story, which is what humans need it to be—and not just any random story, but a particular kind of story. Testimonies always star two central powers, the human and God—both connected, both responsive to each other—and God always wins. The greatest thing about testimonies is that they always end happily, even if they don't. Testimonies are sometimes mocked by unbelievers because some exaggeration of one's past sins and troubles might take place in the service of making a good story better. That would be only natural and would be praised in an Irishman or a poet, but outsiders tend to be hard on evangelicals.

The Tauzins' testimony would be shown on Christmas Eve in a sanctuary that has no crosses, no stained glass, no pews, and none of the high-backed thronelike chairs that preachers in more formal churches sit on. It does have well-padded theater seats. This is a common situation among megachurches, which have often been accused of trying to look like malls. Megachurch pastors count that resemblance as a strength. As an Arizona megachurch pastor once told an interviewer, when people come into his church he hopes it feels so mall-like that they say, "Dude, where's the cinema?"

A control room with glassed-in windows sits high above at the back of the church for controlling cameras and lights. Lighting is important during performances, which feature drums, electronic keyboards, guitars, and singers dressed casually. Pastor Steve usually wears a sport shirt and khakis. There is no choir and nobody wearing robes. Preachers sit in folding chairs like everyone else onstage. Sometimes the stage is decorated with greenery or flowers, but it's the lights that change the mood and setting. They go from rosy to blue hued to hazy white with only a spotlight depending on the mood and situation.

People who aren't accustomed to video screens in church think they make the sermon too impersonal, but the screens are designed to do the opposite. In a room so large, a veritable stadium, the preacher would be just a little man far away without them. Pastor Steve, who began his preaching career long before video came to church, learned to preach by looking at the audience and having it look back at him. He had to learn to look at the cameras, to remember which ones were where, and to give up the idea of feedback. People sitting within feet of him are utterly oblivious to him, their eyes on the screens. It's as though he isn't even there.

Even so, the screens give his sermons intimacy. There's no need to shout. A raised eyebrow, a thoughtful look, the turned-down-edges smile will all be recorded, magnified, turned into something that is easily seen and easily understood. The screens also make him bigger than life, which may not be something his ego demands but is something that our culture does seem to need. Rock stars, movie stars, preachers—they're all in our faces with their huge faces.

It all works. To the visitor, the longtime seeker, the kids who aren't accustomed to church, video screens and theater seating are familiar. The atmosphere says that consumers are welcome to drop in and drop out if they please. Nothing sets apart the people who belong and the people who don't. Nobody will pester you. Nobody will ask for explanations.

The Tauzins' testimony will be a good one for the Christmas Eve service on many points. The Christmas Eve offering at Lake Pointe is a special one, entirely dedicated to the church's benevolence efforts. It brings in the $250,000 that Van Grubbs gives away during the year. Hearing from the Tauzins would remind Lake Pointers of all they had done and would encourage them to do more. They'd done plenty in response to Hurricane Katrina. Lake Pointe sent five trained disaster response teams to the Gulf Coast. Fifty Bible classes "adopted" 168 families, helping them find shelter, work, medical care, transportation, clothing, furniture, and household goods. The church's phone banks helped twelve hundred people locate resources to help them. The Tauzins were among the three hundred families the church ministered to in local hotels and apartments. A tractor trailer was pulled into the church's parking lot and filled with clothing and supplies. Altogether the church raised three hundred thousand dollars and helped eight hundred families through its warehousing efforts. Lake Pointe is also part of the Southern Baptist Convention, which gave $16 million and countless hours of volunteer time to helping areas hit by Katrina damage. The Southern Baptist Convention is the third-largest relief agency in the United States. It was a fine hour for evangelicals.

In the video, however, Pastor Steve won't dwell on all that the church has done materially for the Tauzins. He asked them not to mention that kind of help because it might send the wrong message, the message that getting saved would mean better worldly fortune.

"The Bible says rain falls on the just and the unjust alike," he told me, incorporating biblical language and bits of verse smoothly into his explanation as he often does. "We live in a fallen world. Things won't be perfect until we go to the other world." The grace of Jesus is all that will make up for what humans lose in this life, he said. It is everything and enough.

He wanted the Tauzins to talk about their moment in the hotel conference room and how it changed their lives. He wanted their mud-darkened neighborhood to be the backdrop as the video showed them going into the muck-filled building that was once a home. After a lead-in by him, they would stand in the yard and tell about how they'd dedicated their lives to the Lord.

On the day of filming, as we drove through New Orleans to Chalmette—a neighborhood two miles east of New Orleans, where the Tauzins had lived much of their adult lives—we passed few cars and fewer people, just mile after mile of wrecked housing and abandoned vehicles. Utility repair people were there, police officers and wrecking-company employees and hardly anyone else. Handmade signs advertising demolition services were tacked onto telephone poles at every main corner. A war correspondent who came to New Orleans after the flood said he'd never seen anything as bad as this in war zones. Everything was destroyed; nothing was spared. Street after street, mile after mile after mile of deserted houses. Trees were bare, and there was no grass. Everything was mud colored except swollen pink insulation that had fallen from ceilings and now billowed out windows. Most of the houses would never be salvaged. They'd be bulldozed, but where would all the wreckage go?

The Tauzins' neighborhood was utterly silent, no sound even of birds. The floodwater had risen up to thirty feet and hadn't receded for fourteen days. A half foot of cracked sludge, still toxic with chemicals and oil, covered the yards like a moonscape. *Don't touch anything if you can help it,* we were told, *and if your hand is dirty, don't touch your face.* At their house a white plastic bench rested upside down in the yard, a garden hose snaked across the mud, and an empty Coke can sat tilted in the mire. Its red was startling in a place where everything had turned brown. Next door an air conditioner had floated up to land on the roof. On the way there, we passed a refrigerator perched atop a house.

In the driveway was Michelle's Altima. Inside, the leather was flaked and cracked from having sat in water for days. Their son, eight-year-old Justin, spotted a matted white Teddy bear inside the car. He reached for it, wailing, "Can we get it? I want it."

"No," Michelle told him. "It's ruined."

"That's something my grandmother gave me," he said mournfully.

The smell of mud and rot was mixed with something acrid that began to irritate my nasal passages high up almost behind my eyes. Michelle was holding Justin, his long legs dangling. When she let him down, he was crying and she snuggled his head against her body. He was wearing blue operating-room paper boots that came high on his legs. The rest of us had calf-high rubber boots. Mine were bright pink in honor of New Orleans's indomitable spirit. Everyone else's were black.

"I just wish I could have my bike," Justin said. Then he thought of something else. "My croquet set," he yelled, his voice high and tearful. "I wonder if I can have that. My paw-paw gave me that for my seventh birthday."

He was whimpering between sobs, and Steve put his arm around the boy. Stroope was wearing a denim jacket and a denim shirt that had "Lake Pointe" stitched across the front. His boots were splattered. The lenses of his glasses were the only gleaming objects anywhere. Michelle balanced on one foot as she slid into her boots. Like Justin, she was crying. Justin was now reciting memories of this house where he had lived all his life. His third-birthday party was at the neighborhood McDonalds. He misses friends at his old school.

"You have new friends," Pastor Steve said.

"I just have maybe two," he said.

"Friendly guy like you, you'll make lots of friends."

He nodded, sniffling.

Steve noticed a bandage on Justin's little finger and asked about it.

"My pinky is infected," he said.

Steve spread his broad hands to show that he had his own cuts. "Those are from working in my yard with the palms," he said.

Justin, who is now a regular in Sunday school, said he knew about palms from the story about how the people laid them down before Jesus.

"That's right. Palm Sunday." Steve saw a teachable moment and said, "That was the week before he was crucified."

"That stinks that they crucified him," Justin said. "I wish I could go back and see how they crucified him."

Having tumbled too deeply into an eight-year-old's world for the adult mind to keep up, Steve missed a beat. Justin, a smart boy, glanced at his face and helped him out. "That was sad."

Steve nodded. Thanks to the kid he was back in the game. Yes, it was sad, but Jesus died for our sins, he said. God turned his death into something good

"Just like the hurricane," Steve said. "God's going to turn this into something good."

Michelle went first into the house, pushing the blocked door open enough to slide through. Inside, furniture, turned upside down and sideways, was piled in rotting heaps. The floor was so caked and squishy that it couldn't be seen at all. There was no place to get good footing. The hall was blocked by rubble and impossible to get through. The only thing standing was the brick column where the kitchen stove had been. Everything else had floated and banged together, rotted and collapsed into itself. By the time I edged in, Michelle was at the back of the house.

She was moaning, "Oh. Oh. Oh. Thank you, God. Thank you, God."

She was crying hard enough that I could hear her breath coming in fast, whimpery puffs. It was hard to see how she got there. Climbing over a desk seemed to be the only way forward, and that looked dangerous—as if anyone trying it might step down into thigh-high grime or fall elbow deep into the trash. One of the church cameramen was near her, filming. Neither Pastor Steve nor I was too keen to follow. He, at least, asked how to and eventually worked his way forward. I contented myself with looking on. Preachers have to wade into the mire. We reporters just watch.

She was crying because she had found an album of her own baby pictures.

"Look, look," she called out. "They're all right. They're still all right. I can't believe I found them. Thank you, God. Thank you, God."

It might seem an odd moment to envy Michelle, but I did. She was able to touch God amid the mud, claim the promises, grasp the very evidence of Almighty power. Perhaps you're scoffing at Michelle's joy. *Baby pictures?* you're thinking. *That's all God gave back? Better if he'd taken stronger action, like diverting the hurricane and letting the Tauzin family go on with their lives.* But that's not how evangelicals think, as the Tauzins are learning. God worked his wondrous ways that the Tauzins might come to know him and be saved. Knowing him, obeying him, seeing his presence in life—that's all that matters. Clutch that and it will be true. Not only for the Tauzins, but for all the victims of

Katrina and all the victims of life's ills everywhere. I once heard Billy Graham say that he didn't worry about anything because he lived in God's will and anything God brought him would be what he wanted in his life. That's a fine place to be.

Michelle later told me that she once would have called finding those baby pictures good fortune, a coincidence, or luck, as the rest of us do, but now she knows it as a blessing from God. Making the leap from a life that's random to one that features God's guidance, messages, and gifts is a crucial step in building and living evangelical faith. Lake Pointe will cement Michelle's new perceptions by mirroring and affirming them as reality. Her world now resembles the world inhabited by most of humankind for most of history. A benevolent force listens to her, cares for her, and responds regularly to help her.

The mundane has become holy. She will now be able to summon the very presence of God with her prayers. She will feel him with her. I remember that feeling well and sometimes still have it. It is as if a calming presence has descended. Someone is listening. She will now feel protected and be able to help protect others. She will no longer be helpless in the face of misery. While the rest of us have only the puny aid of good energy or positive thoughts, she will access a link with limitless power. Like an old woman looking at youth, I listened as she praised God, and I thought, "How beautiful. How lucky she is. I remember being like that."

After an hour or so, the Tauzins, Pastor Steve, and the cameramen moved to the side of the house to stand under the leafless tree in what was left of the front yard to tape their testimony. Before the camera began rolling, Steve told them that they were to put events in their own words and to be patient; they might have to retell the stories several times. I wondered if Mike would say much. Fishing was the only subject I'd seen that opened him up. He'd told Steve how after work each night he could walk just yards from his New Orleans house and start fishing. He'd talked about what kind of fish he caught and the kind of fish they resembled and the kind of fight they put up. Mike is unlikely to ever again have fishing so close at hand, and he'd spoken of it with sadness. But I didn't need to worry about his willingness to talk for the camera. Thanks to Lake Pointe, Mike has something he didn't have before.

"We found our faith," he said of that day at the Holiday Inn.

"We always believed in God, but we didn't practice," said Michelle.

"We didn't love his Word," said Mike.

"We're not ready to say this yet, but someday I hope we will say it was the best thing that ever happened to us because we found our faith," said Michelle. "I cried often. I was a mess. But God bottled up my tears."

"She used to worry all the time," said Mike, "phone calls all the time and up in the middle of the night. Now you've just got to trust in God."

She has had insomnia for a month and half. At first she worried that she would never sleep again. Then she realized "when it's God's time for me to sleep I would sleep."

Mike said of the church people, "They were a blessing to us, and they say we were a blessing to them."

"That's how it works," Steve said

"Everyone practiced what they preached," Michelle said. "I've lived all over the world. My dad was in the military. And I've never met anyone like them."

Shifting gears, Steve said, "Well, guys, the last Christmas you had was in this house."

Mike came in as if on cue: "This will be the first time Christ will really be in our Christmas." When Michelle sent out Christmas cards this year, she underlined the *Christ* in *Christmas*. "Because that's what it's about," she told the camera.

While the Tauzins were filming, a neighbor couple drove up. Afterward, Michelle went over to talk with the woman, who was small and had a mass of dark, curly hair. Michelle planned to let the government bulldoze their house, but the neighbors hoped to salvage their house and move back in. Since the hurricane, doctors had discovered the wife has a brain tumor.

Michelle asked if Pastor Steve could come over to pray. They stood in a huddle with their arms around each other's shoulders, heads bowed. Steve said a few more words after the prayer, taking all the time he needed, but then he moved away. Michelle started telling the former neighbor about how wonderful the church is and how she and Mike had been saved and how they're reading the Bible now and how much different and better their lives are.

The woman was polite. She nodded repeatedly. "That's good. That's good," she said, keeping her eyes focused on her house. Michelle kept talking about her new life with Christ in the way anyone does when saying something important that's not being heard. She was trying to find words to express how big this change was, but such mysteries can't be put into words. So Michelle wrapped it up with a hug.

"I love you, girl. We'll see each other again."

"We'll be all right," the neighbor said, glancing at Michelle and then away. "We'll be all right." Like me, like millions of others who hear the Good News that evangelicals offer, she was polite, perhaps grateful for the prayers, but she wasn't buying.

End of chpt. 3

Chpt.
Four) goes to pg. 66

IN THE YEAR OF "EVERYONE CAN!" EVERYONE DIDN'T

Evangelical salvation still packs a punch. As Mike and Michelle Tauzins' story shows, it still transforms lives and brings believers into churches more ready to receive them and better able to serve them than ever before. Membership has no dues. No fees. No pressure. Evangelicals ought to be pulling converts in as fast as they can park their cars.

Common wisdom says they are. For years, evangelicals and their theological brethren, Pentecostals and charismatics, have been the only success story in American Christianity. Only they can report that they are growing by converting the lost, but what most people don't know is that the increase is tiny. Southern Baptist growth was down to 0.02 percent in 2005 and is still dropping. Pentecostal churches are generally so small that their growth may look good in percentage terms but not so impressive in absolute numbers. The biggest of those churches and the country's leader in percentage growth is the Assemblies of God at 2.8 million. They add about fifty thousand members a year, making them far and away the biggest Protestant winner. At a growth rate of 1.86 they exceed the U.S. population growth rate of 1.3, but they have a long way to go before they'll be a political and social force. (If you apply our Sunday school rule to them, they have an active membership of only seven hundred thousand.) What makes both denominations look really good is comparison with the so-called mainline churches—Methodists, Presbyterians, Episcopalians, Lutherans—who are all losing members and have been for years. It is no exaggeration to say that the fate of Protestant Christianity in America hangs on the success of the evangelicals. If they aren't making it, neither is Western Christianity. That the United States might go the way of Western Europe, where Christianity is so irrelevant that U.S. evangelicals send missionaries there, is a pressing concern among church leaders and seems more likely each year.

Evangelicals and their politicians see themselves as the last bulkhead in a war against secularism. A large part of their power comes from the fact that in the last thirty years it seemed that the only way for a church to grow was to do exactly what Lake Pointe Church, the Southern Baptist Convention, and independent evangelical churches have done: be literalist about the Bible, adhere to the most conservative religious standards, and invest great spiritual authority in leadership rather than in the individual discernment of laypeople.[1] Such evangelicals commonly adhere to a list of fundamentals that are among the touchstones most of us think of when defining modern-day evangelicals. They include:

- The inerrancy of Scripture

- The virgin birth and the deity of Jesus

- The bodily resurrection of Jesus

- The idea that salvation and atonement for sin come only through the death of Jesus, God's grace, and human faith

- The imminent second coming of Christ

This list is one that a group of conservative American Christians put together about a hundred years ago and called the fundamentals of Christianity. They called themselves the *fundamentalists,* which was the first religious use of that term. Those standards have helped make Southern Baptists the country's biggest Protestant denomination, and they've helped make the Assemblies of God the country's fastest-growing in percentage terms.

That helps to explain why politicians outside the evangelical camp have seen their faith treated as though it were of no value whatsoever. Mainline denominations, such as the Episcopal, Presbyterian, Methodist, and Lutheran churches, and even progressive evangelicals, such as former president Jimmy Carter and former vice president Al Gore, have come to be seen as weak and ineffective. I'm leaving out former president Bill Clinton for obvious reasons, but he, too, is a progressive evangelical, and as I write this, he and former president Carter are trying to bring evangelicals together around some of the primary moral concerns of mainline Christians—social ills such as poverty, injustice, racism, and violence. These issues have been branded as liberal and lacking in importance because of the hegemony that the religious right has exercised over moral discourse in America. The religious right has elevated sexual issues to the forefront even though most of America is less concerned than it has ever been about other people's sexual behavior. They've been able to do this because again and again the most conservative of evangelicals have made the headlines while other Christians, who are actually the majority of American Christians, have become more and more invisible.

At the beginning of this book, I mentioned that evangelicals and those who benefit by exaggerating their power have understood media weaknesses and exploited them brilliantly. Just how brilliantly was demonstrated in a recent study by a media watchdog group called Media Matters for America. It showed that conservative religious causes and spokesmen are featured nearly three times more often in television and print reports than moderate and progressive Christians.[2]

"That exposure explains how and why the right's pet issues define public religious discourse and shape conventional wisdom about the 'culture wars,'" writes Diane Winston, a former religion reporter who holds the Knight Chair in Religion and Media at the University of Southern California. Journalists have come to see "religious orthodoxy as the authentic religious voice" of America, she adds.

The religious right began framing the news agenda in the 1980s. The Institute for Religion and Democracy, a religious-right think tank, launched a two-pronged campaign to defund and delegitimate Protestant moderates and progressives, a process that has been well documented by historians and alternative-press journalists. First they began fomenting dissention over gender and sexuality inside the mainline churches. Their efforts sparked decades of interdenominational battles that kept news coverage focused on those issues only. Everything else about those denominations was effectively ignored. The second prong of the attack, writes Winston, was to accuse mainline churches, especially the National Council of Churches, of being soft on Communism. When the *Reader's Digest*, the *Wall Street Journal*, and *60 Minutes* did stories that charged ecumenical leaders with supporting and funding Marxist guerrillas, liberation theology, and other Communist fronts in the developing world, mainline churches were effectively neutralized.

But, Winston notes, the real squeeze came after 9-11, when "the Bush administration yoked American politics to the conservative Christian project, a linkage most of the press uncritically and unquestioningly repeated for nearly five years." Why? Partly, she says, because the press echoed the post–9-11 political climate, and partly because they didn't understand the importance of religion well enough to know what they were doing. "Cowed by leaders who spoke as true believers and wary of offending readers and viewers, the press fell into line," she writes.[3]

As a result, the most conservative of the evangelicals have been seen as unchallenged winners in the religious marketplace. They said they had huge numbers. Robust growth. Unswerving devotion. They *seemed* invincible. And they would be if any of that were true. But, as we've already seen, it is not. Their numbers are about a fourth of what they are supposed to be. Their growth is flagging. Once again, don't take my word for it. These contentions are too radical to be taken on faith. I've shown you the great rewards that Michelle and Mike Tauzin are getting from evangelical belief. Now let me show you a set of facts that, in light of the Tauzins' experience, seem mystifying.

As a prelude, I want to debunk one of the most common misconceptions about the direction that spirituality is moving in the United States. Evangelicals are not the fastest-growing faith group in America. Neither are Pentecostals. Nonbelievers are the fastest-growing faith group in America in numbers and percentage. From 1990 to 2001, which was the last good count, they more than doubled, from 14 million to 29 million. Their proportion of the population grew from 8 percent to more than 14 percent. That means there are more than twice as many people who claim no religion as there are participating evangelicals who subscribe to beliefs that have made the religious right powerful.[4]

Why hasn't the growth of nonbelievers been given the mainstream media play that the false estimation of evangelical power has been given? Because there are no powerful groups that benefit by keeping it in the news. With no constituency pushing the concerns of this group into public view or deliberately shaping the media agenda so that its concerns seem more widespread than they are, stories that represent the rapidly growing group of nonbelievers flash briefly into view and then disappear long before they can make an impact on public consciousness. One reporter can do a story. It might be picked up by other reporters, but without other forces at work it's a one-day wonder. Groups of atheists do not gather to protest or to stage antiprayer rallies. People who oppose religion are likely to remain silent rather than express views that will offend others. A hint about the large number of nonbelievers did capture the press's attention recently when three new books hit the bestseller lists portraying religious belief as not only wrong but positively evil. This new, more aggressive form of nonbelief is being called the New Atheism and could develop a constituency, but it's not likely.

Another story that flashed briefly into view and faded without affecting public perception one whit came from a Pew Forum on Religion and Public Life study in 2004 that showed "other" Christians make up 67 percent of the U.S. population, while traditionalist evangelicals (who would be core religious-right evangelicals) make up only 12.6 percent of the population. That means that there are five times more non-religious-right Christians than there are religious-right Christians.

Who are these "other" Christians?

The first group will surprise you. They are moderate and progressive evangelicals. These non-religious-right evangelicals actually outnumber religious-right evangelicals by 1 percent. Then there are Catholics, other Protestants, and Christians who don't fit into any of the main groupings. Granted, some of them are identified in the study as traditionalists. But when we look at what this self-identification study meant by traditionalists, the religious-right numbers get even weaker. For evangelical Protestants, traditionalists were those who claimed to be fundamentalist, evangelical, Pentecostal, or charismatic, and others who agreed on the need to preserve religious traditions. All of those who agree on the need to preserve religious traditions are certainly not members of the religious right, but when the researchers turned to mainline Protestants (Episcopalians, Methodists, Lutherans, Presbyterians) they used that criterion alone as a way of categorizing someone as traditionalist.

But once again, let's give the religious right every benefit of the doubt. Even if you add mainline Protestants who want to preserve religious traditions and consider them religious-right supporters, you've only got 17 percent in the religious-right camp. Other Christians, the great mainstream of American Christians, still outnumber them almost four to one. But anyone reading the media would never believe that. In fact, when I told my mainstream Christian friends that they and their kind vastly outnumber religious-right Christians, not one of them believed me. So I quoted the statistics. In response, they generally looked confused, as if they couldn't quite comprehend such a radical notion. The majority of American Christians have been so marginalized by public rhetoric and news coverage that they don't even know they are the overwhelming majority of Christians and that they are the Christians who actually represent American religious values, not the religious right.

Why does hardly anyone know these statistics? Once again, because there is no organized, concentrated campaign to create media and get power by using them. Few media outlets picked up on that aspect of the study. And those that did, didn't trumpet the results. Didn't make the front pages. Didn't make the talk shows. This story wasn't even a one-day wonder. It almost didn't exist.

By influencing media coverage and eventually the public's perception of truth, conservative evangelicals created the kind of distortion that caused historian Daniel Boorstin to call ours the "era of contrivance." Once we understand evangelical numbers in context, we begin to understand that America is a very different place than many of us have been led to believe it is. And

Americans themselves are a very different kind of people. More thoughtful. More reasoning. Less doctrinaire. More changeable. More flexible. Less religious. If our governmental policies don't reflect those qualities, a big reason may be that our politicians have been misled, along with the rest of us.

THE REVEREND BOBBY Welch was certainly aware that Southern Baptists were not in the splendid shape they seemed to be when he took over as president of the Southern Baptist Convention in 2004. Welch also knew a fact that rarely makes media stories about evangelical growth: Southern Baptist growth isn't keeping up with population growth, and it hasn't for years.

Here's how that fact gets so easily ignored. When comparisons are made, they're usually between evangelicals and Presbyterian, Lutheran, Methodist, and Episcopal mainline Christians. If it's a race between those two groups, evangelicals are clearly winning. But the real race is between evangelicals and the rest of the country. If the population is growing faster than evangelicals are, they are losing to the competition that counts. They are weakening as their opponent, worldly allure, gains strength. The distance between them and cultural victory grows every day that they are outpaced by population, and every day the United States becomes a less Christian nation. For evangelicals, this is a life-and-death fight. They either win or they lose. There's no in between.

Welch knew that dramatic action was needed, and since Southern Baptists estimate that 200 million Americans are unsaved, he also knew that the potential harvest, to use a common evangelical metaphor, could be vast. To make his million-baptism goal in one year, all Southern Baptists had to do was convince one out of every two hundred unsaved Americans to be baptized. Considering all that evangelical faith offers, how hard could that be?

If you ask Americans whether they believe in the fundamental matters of faith that Southern Baptists cling to, the majority will agree with most of them. If you ask evangelicals what brings people to Christ, they'll say the transformed lives of believers. With most of America already convinced on matters of faith and thousands of churches filled with transformed people like the Tauzins, eager to tell others of their new life, how hard could it be to convert one out of two hundred lost people? How hard could that be for a faith that is so widely portrayed as more powerful politically, socially, and economically than ever in its history? How hard could that be for a denomination that is so expert at evangelizing that unbelievers wince at merely hearing the name?

Southern Baptist churches are soul-saving machines. Hard sell? Soft sell? They can do it. Always good at it, they've only gotten better since I left so many years ago. They've boiled down escape from everlasting hellfire to four simple spiritual laws that can be summarized in a pamphlet, memorized, and delivered even as a door is closing on your foot. Southern Baptists study how to witness, rehearse how to do it, and recap having done it. Their preachers pray about it loudly. They preach about it often. They plan for it constantly. The simple methods of my child-hood—pack the pews night after night during weeklong revivals and endlessly croon stanzas of "Nothing but the Blood of Jesus" as the preachers plead with sinners to come down the aisle—are old style now. Today's savvy ministers bring the saved and un-saved together with tennis tournaments, golf outings, and soft-ball teams; with business luncheons, business networking, leadership groups, and financial counseling; with marriage en-counter weekends, movie nights, and musical events featuring nationally known performers. Almost everything is free.

These events make it easy to evangelize. Believers don't have to make a pitch for Jesus that might embarrass them and alien-ate their friends. They don't even have to invite people to a church service. Instead, they can say, "Let's have some fun to-gether" or "I'm going to a workshop that might help you with your business [family, finances]," and the event just happens to be at a church. At the same time the most successful churches, Lake Pointe among them, make sure such invitations will be forthcoming by asking believers to sign yearly pledges naming specific people whom they will pray for, witness to, and invite to church that year. These pledges are printed on wallet-sized cards to be carried right alongside photos of the family.

In seven years, one seventy-three-year-old Baptist woman in Statesville, North Carolina, has caused more than two thousand people to pray the prayer of acceptance, which is evangelical shorthand for being born again. In nursing homes, at food pantries, at soup kitchens, at the county fair, in the hospital recovering from a fall that she blames on the devil's interference, Nell Kerley converts sinners to Christians. She learned how to do it in her Sunday school class, and hardly a day has gone by since without her inviting someone to be saved. During her hospital stay, she saved nineteen people. "The devil thought he had me," she said. "But he threw me in the right briar patch, just like Br'er Rabbit." After the hospital released her, she went back for a visit and six more people prayed for salvation.

She stopped converting patients only when a patient's spouse complained and she was barred from proselytizing on the premises. She's a bit like a bulldog, another Baptist said. When one unsaved woman told Nell she would rather go to hell than give up her men, the Baptist said, "Well, honey, you're on your way there."[5]

Nell does more than most Southern Baptists, but her methods are standard for doing God's business the Baptist way. On the surface, these methods are working well for evangelicals. They make a great story. But note one thing about Nell Kerley's efforts: she gets them to accept Jesus and pray, but she doesn't get them to join a church. I know from living in the South most of my life that it isn't so hard to get a southerner to accept Jesus.

They'll do that just to be polite—if not to you, to Jesus. But getting them to commit to a church is a lot harder.

Daytona Beach pastor and SBC president Bobby Welch knew that even better than I do. So he wanted more than conversions, he wanted baptisms, which show that a convert has followed through and usually that someone has joined a church. Welch issued a breathtakingly bold challenge: a million baptisms in one year—almost three times what Southern Baptist churches were doing when he took office. This was no amateur, uncoordinated effort. The plan for Welch's Everyone Can! Kingdom Challenge was that the churches would get on their mark in 2004, get set in 2005, and race toward a million souls in 2006.

Pastor Welch, a former Green Beret, went at it with all his considerable might. In a twenty-one-day road tour, he logged twenty thousand miles and visited all fifty states, riding in a special bus that had the American flag and faces of Southern Baptists painted on the sides. Messages emblazoned across the bus read "Everyone Can Witness, Win and Baptize . . . One Million!" and "Do all you can . . . with all you have . . . where you are . . . NOW!" At each church he visited, Welch showed the way by joining church members as they went door-to-door witnessing. In his wake, Southern Baptists led prayer walks through neighborhoods, did more door-to-door visits, buttonholed people at their jobs, and preached at them in the streets. They went to universities, they went to inner cities, they held block parties in the suburbs. They hit the rodeos and ball fields. They gave away food. They traveled to disaster sites giving out aid and the Gospel.

When the figures were in, the news was bad. Baptisms were down for the fourth year out of five. They had declined by 4.15 percent to 371,850, causing one headline quip in Tennessee: "In the year of Everyone Can, everyone didn't." Southern Baptists made their best effort and baptized fewer people than they had in 1950. When Baptist researchers recently went looking for any church that was performing as well as the average Southern Baptist Church fifty years ago, out of forty-three hundred churches they found only twenty-two.[6]

And that isn't even the worst of it. Once again, to understand how bad things really are, we've got to delve more deeply into what that baptism count means. I've said that baptism is more reliable than merely a count of those who've said they accept Jesus, but in another way, a baptism count can be deceptive. Anyone who didn't understand Baptists might think those baptisms are a count of sinners' conversions to Christianity. But they aren't.

Christians can be saved only once, according to Baptist belief, but they can be baptized more than once. Only those baptized by immersion can be Southern Baptists. Christians who were baptized as infants or as adults by having water sprinkled over them or Pentecostals who were baptized by the holy spirit, which is speaking in tongues, and were not totally immersed in water would not be accepted in a Baptist church as properly baptized. If a Catholic or a Methodist, for instance, joins a Baptist church, that person may have already been christened as a baby, which is a form of baptism that marks the child's salvation and status as a Christian. In that process, water is merely sprinkled over the child. Later the child will go through training in basics of the faith and have a confirmation that reaffirms he is part of the Christian community.

But Baptists believe people must first confess that they are sinners and accept the forgiveness of Christ, a process that may be referred to in many ways: being born again, or accepting salvation, or making a decision for Christ, or becoming a Christian. Sometimes is it even called walking the aisle or answering the call, because traditionally Baptists and other evangelical preachers issue "an altar call" or invitation to salvation at the end of each service. People who want to become Christians or join the church walk down the aisle or "come forth publicly," as many Baptists put it, which is important to them because it follows the biblical injunction to confess your faith before men. Infants, of course, are not able to do this. Most Baptists accept that people from other denominations are Christians if they have confessed their sins and accepted Christ, but to belong to a Baptist church these other Christians must be baptized in the Baptist way, which is called full immersion.

All Baptist churches have a baptismal pool. The preacher and the convert walk into the pool until the water is at or above their waists, and as the preacher says, "I baptize you in the name of the Father, Son, and the Holy Spirit," he puts one hand on the person's face, often holding the nose, and another hand on the convert's back at waist level, dipping the convert backward until the water is completely over his head. Then the preacher raises him up out of the water and welcomes him into the newness of life in Christ.

What all this means when counting baptisms is that any Southern Baptist count of baptisms would not be a count of only people who had been unsaved and now were saved. Instead it could include many Christians already saved and baptized in other churches. Why does this matter? It matters because Baptists and other evangelicals might seem to be making a great number of conversions when actually they were only "trading the sheep" or "shuffling the saints," as it's often termed. If all you want is a bigger church and we're just talking about one church, it doesn't matter in the short term. But evangelicals are charged with bringing the world to salvation. They must convert sinners in order to fulfill their commission from God. The vigor of evangelical life hinges on converting others. If Baptists are mainly stealing Christians from other denominations, their growth is not the growth of Christian belief at all, but merely a shifting from one form of Christianity to another. To put it in economic terms, the evangelicals are getting people to shift brands but they aren't penetrating new markets.

To see their problem, we might compare it to selling laundry soap. At one time, almost everyone washed their clothes with laundry soap. Those are the Christians. Some people didn't wash their clothes. Those are the sinners. There were many brands of laundry soap and competition among them. A laundry-soap maker expanded his market by convincing sinners to wash and Christians to switch brands. But then detergent was invented. (In our little parable, detergent stands in for many things: people who are "spiritual but not religious," secularism, other religions, and so forth. It's the new competition. We'll discuss that aspect of the faith picture in more depth later.) So now among the non–soap users there were people who didn't wash and people who washed with detergent and were teaching their children to wash with detergent. Some laundry-soap makers did better than others by convincing more soap users that their laundry soap was superior. But if the number of people using detergent and the number of people who don't wash their clothes continues to grow faster than the number of new laundry-soap users, the laundry-soap makers are doomed.

That's exactly where evangelical churches are finding themselves. The evidence comes from Southern Baptists' own studies. Only 7 percent of members who've been in a Southern Baptist church five years or less are true converts, meaning sinners who weren't raised in the church but came in through a profession of faith in Jesus, according to Southern Baptist records. If you took out the Southern Baptists who married unbelievers and brought them to faith, hardly anybody would be left. Hartford Institute for Religion Research researcher Scott Thumma's study of a charismatic nondenominational megachurch showed something similar. While 27 percent of the church's members said they were new Christians, only 7 percent had grown up without a church or in a non-Christian faith.[7] So who are the other 93 percent of church members? Once again, Southern Baptists have the numbers.

Twenty percent are Christians who have already been dunked in other Baptist churches. Another 40 percent are Christians who have already been sprinkled, which is baptism by the non-Baptist way. Twenty-six percent are children in vacation Bible school.[8] To go back to our analogy again, these are children who've been convinced to use laundry soap. Many come from homes that don't wash or use detergent. They may become life-long laundry-soap users, but this is an iffy market. Sometimes children convince the whole family to begin using laundry soap, but it's more likely that the children will use laundry soap for a time and then return to the ways of their families.

That's 86 percent of baptisms coming from Christians (people who already use laundry soap) and children (an unstable market). The detergent market, meanwhile, and the number of people who don't wash is doubling, attracting the young and converting laundry-soap users of all brands. I've made my point with the analogy. I'll drop it now.

Bringing children to faith is important, and "trading the sheep" can mean a great renewal of faith, as it did with the Tauzins, but as a growth strategy it's troublesome, especially for the evangelicals. With the population and the churches aging, there are going to be fewer children to convert. As other Christian groups lose members, there are going to be fewer sheep to trade.

Now we're left with only 14 percent of all baptisms. There's trouble there, too. Baptisms are going down in every age group except children under five. For a snapshot of the situation, let's look at young adults, a critical group. In the eighteen-to-thirty-four age group, Southern Baptist baptisms fell 40 percent, from one hundred thousand in 1980 to sixty thousand in 2005.[9] This is dire news on two fronts. Late adolescence is a time of great emotional tension and change, when conversion offers a life plan and purpose, something young people seek and need as they move into adulthood. Conversions at this point often yield deep, lifelong commitments. The second reason this age group is important for conversions is that young families, which are forming in great numbers from ages eighteen to thirty-four, are fertile ground for conversion. Evangelicals marry and bring spouses of other faiths into the church to be baptized. Couples of different backgrounds become seekers looking for a church they can both be comfortable in. During these prime childbearing ages, the push to find a church is especially intense. A 40 percent drop in this critical, core population is devastating news in another way also. Energetic young families with rising incomes are the lifeblood of growing churches. A drop in their numbers could be catastrophic.

If you recall that Southern Baptists are far and away the biggest evangelical group in the country, almost six times bigger than their nearest evangelical competition, you can see that their trouble is everybody's trouble. A look at the biggest growth story in evangelical circles, the Assemblies of God, confirms that. Their Pentecostal practices helped them expand adherents from 1.8 million in 1980 to nearly 2.8 million in 2004. Among Pentecostals, baptism—either by immersion in water or by the Holy Spirit, which as mentioned means receiving the gift of speaking in tongues—is crucial. The number of people who have received either baptism has been 175,000 to 200,000 each year—a half to a third less than the 371,000 the Baptists are bringing in.

The truth behind all these numbers is that evangelicals are not converting and cannot convert non-Christian adult Americans, especially native-born white people, in significant numbers. Almost all the recent growth in Southern Baptist numbers has come from the very people who gave evangelicals their start, people on the margins of middle-class life. African-Americans and Hispanics are some part of that growth, which is why the Southern Baptist Convention is turning increasing attention to people of color in the United States and abroad. What that means is that white Republican evangelicals, the group that defines evangelical faith in the public mind, are not gaining ground, as many people think they are. They're losing it.

Bobby Welch knows that. He called the failure of his crusade to baptize a million people "the most urgent cry Southern Baptists will ever hear" and said it came from the handwriting now on the wall. For most people "handwriting on the wall" is merely a cliché, but for Southern Baptists, among the most biblically literate people in the world, it means much more. The handwriting Dr. Welch was referring to came from a story in the biblical book of Daniel. A hand appeared during a banquet and wrote words on the wall as King Belshazzar and his guests were drinking from goblets stolen out of the Jewish temple. Neither the king nor his wise men knew what the words meant. On advice from his wife, King Belshazzar sent for Daniel, who was among the Jews being held captive. Daniel told the king that the words meant "God has numbered the days of your reign and brought it to an end. You have been weighed in the scales and found wanting. Your kingdom is to be divided and given to the Medes and Persians." A chilling message for King Belshazzar and for evangelicals in America.

End g clpt. 4

66,

- chpt. 5 -

chpt
Five ⟩ *goes to pg 78*

PRAYING FOR A MIRACLE

Before I tell you another story from inside the evangelical church, let me recap what we know. Organized special-interest groups have manipulated news reports, created conflicts, and inflated statistics so convincingly that the face of American religion—in fact, the image of America itself—has been distorted. A small and declining group of people has been portrayed as tremendously powerful and growing so rapidly that they might take over the country—when in fact the number of converts among this group is down and dropping. They are rarely able to convert an adult, middle-class American. Their share of the population is not 25 percent but at most 7 percent of the country and falling. All these numbers come from the churches themselves.

As a contrast to those figures, I've taken you inside the evangelical church with two stories of faith. These stories are examples of the great virtue that ultraconservative evangelical faith still has. I've cited them as reasons to wonder why so many people are rejecting a faith that delivers so much. In Van Grubbs's story, we saw evangelical faith doing good works through a man who believes that God speaks directly to him. His life has meaning, purpose, and certainties beyond what most of us can even hope for. Then we looked at Katrina refugees Michelle and Mike Tauzins' conversion and saw their lives transformed. Although my intent in both these stories was to point out the virtues of religious-right faith, some readers will have made their own judgments about the "vices" I referred to as part of what is killing this type of faith. These readers will probably find more "vices" in my next story. I won't give them any help. Yet.

The story I'm about to tell answers a question that must be addressed in any thorough examination of ultraconservative evangelical faith. Can their God actually rescue the faithful? We've seen that Van Grubbs believes his God to be powerful. We've seen in the lives of Michelle and Mike Tauzin how a convert might come to believe that. But we've yet to see otherworldly actions that might convince us, which brings us to the story of Mark and Susan Bruk.

Through her faith, Susan Bruk has obtained what philosopher Friedrich Nietzsche, no friend to Christianity but a fearless thinker anyway, calls the greatest power any human can have. She has turned great pain into something good. She has been able to do what Solzhenitsyn did with his time in the Soviet gulags, what Dostoyevsky did with his escape from a death sentence and ten years in Siberia, what Elie Wiesel did with the death of his family and his own suffering in Nazi concentration camps. Her faith put Susan Bruk—midwestern mother of three, singer of Christian songs—among the greats of history, able to turn tragedy into triumph, and able to show others how to do the same. At the risk of being tedious, I'll repeat what I've said in the previous two stories. It would be reasonable to expect that a line of eager acolytes would be forming at her door. The mystery is that it isn't.

• • •

WHEN DOCTORS SAID only a miracle could keep forty-two-year-old Mark Bruk alive, they must have meant that as a warning. Mark and his wife, Susan, didn't hear it that way. Being in this world but not of this world, they didn't have to. God does miracles. He would do one for them. Hundreds of prayer warriors—dedicated, consecrated, devoted, as Susan and Mark were, as they had been their entire lives—were praying for Mark's recovery. Deacons had laid hands on him and called for healing. Two of the staunchest, most powerful of the Christians in their seven-thousand-member evangelical Wisconsin church had been in sustained communication with God about Mark, and they said God had told them that he was going to be healed.

Mark Bruk was a strapping, healthy guy when one day he complained of a bad stomachache. It got worse. X rays showed cancer. Who could blame the Bruks if they had asked, "Why Mark? Why this father of three young children, God? Why such a good man when so many evil men were flourishing?" That was the first temptation. But the Bruks, married fifteen years, serving the Lord always, didn't ask.

Their happiness had been hard-won. Susan was sure that Mark was God's choice for her long before they married. Mark was not so sure. So she prayed, and he prayed, and for five and a half years they ended each date with nothing more than a kiss. Susan's friends told her to move on, but "he was so kind and gentle," she said. "I thought, *This is what Jesus must have been like.*" So she wouldn't give up, and finally, one Christmas, Mark asked her to marry him. They prayed together after he gave her the ring, asking the Lord to bless their marriage. And he did. They had three healthy children and a good living.

When Mark had that stomachache checked out, biopsies showed a rare type of cancer caused by exposure to asbestos.

Mark had never worked with asbestos, but there it was. Many people are exposed to asbestos in the course of their lives, but they don't get cancer. Mark did. That was the second time anyone might have doubted God's good plan. Mark and Susan didn't.

Unlike other cancers that form compact tumors, this one spread over his stomach like moss and then moved to other organs. Soon after his diagnosis, it simply exploded. Mark had seven surgeries in two months. Infection set in. Trying to keep it under control, doctors left his stomach open. When they wanted to close it finally, the skin around the wound had so dried out that it wouldn't stretch. Susan believed that God was letting things get worse, letting Satan have his way, so he could show his glory with a miracle. It was a test, like Job had been put to, and like Job, she and Mark would pass it, still faithful to God.

Then the doctors came to say that Mark would die that day or the next. Susan was so shocked that the muscles in her jaw went slack. Looking into Mark's eyes, she saw the same shock. How could this be true? Then the doctors—Susan still calls them the death doctors—asked an odd question: "How are you feeling?" Mark's mouth was so swollen and bloody that it was hard to understand him, but there was no mistaking his response this time.

"I'm excited to see Jesus," he said.

When they were alone, Susan told him a few things she was sorry for. One was having been so grumpy in the mornings. Mark told her none of that mattered.

"I made a good decision," he said. She knew that he meant marrying her had not been a mistake. Then he asked her to kiss him on the lips.

She pulled the breathing mask from his face and gave him a last kiss. She called his family and his friends in to say good-bye to him. Later that day he fell into unconsciousness. At one point, she was beside his bed singing one of their favorite songs, "Christ the Lord Is Risen Today." Just as she was belting out a part that she and Mark's sister had added to the middle—"Shout the battle's won, Christ, the Risen Lord, He's our victory"— Mark opened his eyes for the last time. Susan now believes it was in that moment that Mark saw Jesus and went home to heaven.

Susan didn't think that at the time. She still believed that God would pull it out. But he didn't. Mark died the next day, on a Sunday morning, two months after his diagnosis. Susan, alone with him, had been in the room about five minutes when his heart rate plummeted from 120 beats per minute to zero.

"It was so nice of God to let me be there," she told me. As others who loved Mark came into the room, they circled his body and thanked God for having known Mark. Then they made a vow. "Satan," they said, raising their clasped hands high, "you will get nothing from us. We are going to follow God with more fervor than ever."

For three days, Susan held to the hope that God would restore life to Mark's body. He'd done that with Jesus, and he could do it again if he wanted to. Susan thought he would want to. But he didn't. After the third day, she gave up. God had allowed Satan to triumph for a reason. God would let her know why when she got to heaven.

I first saw Susan Bruk a year later at a Christmas presentation for women in Brookfield, Wisconsin, where I lived then. Her church, Elmbrook, is the most well known evangelical church in the area, so renowned that its members are sometimes referred to by a nickname: Brookies. The name is not always said with pleasure. Sometimes people roll their eyes or grimace. Other times they are overly careful when they say the church's name, waiting to hear who's in the group before commenting further. I've heard Elmbrook Church described as both a cult and a great blessing to the community.

Those who disapprove love telling stories about church members' transgressions. One person swears that drugs are dealt by some people in the congregation, which sounds pretty terrible. But since anyone who wants to go to church is free to do so and evangelical churches make special efforts for teens, that could be true and not be a particularly black mark. I've also heard that Elmbrook requires members to turn over their tax returns so leaders can monitor whether members are giving enough. Not true. I've heard that Elmbrook is the best place in town to make business connections, which is the main reason people go there. I've heard that teenagers go there only because it's the cool church.

All this is to say that Elmbrook, like evangelical megachurches all over the country, is located amid the kind of medium-sized, fast-growing, prosperous suburbs that don't have a lot to gossip about. Elmbrook Church looms large in the imagination and affairs of the communities around it. Its money, the array of programs it offers, the size of its buildings—even the size of its parking lots—inspire envy. "Have you seen that place?" my neighbors often asked when the name *Elmbrook* was mentioned. "Have you seen the traffic on Sunday mornings?" It looks like a mall surrounded by acres of parking, which makes it typical of megachurches. They rely on technology, programming, and unyielding theology rather than spires or awesome architecture to give people a taste of the Lord.

The passion that some of Elmbrook's evangelical members display is intense enough to raise outsiders' ire. When one of my Methodist neighbors heard that a friend was leaving the Catholic church for Elmbrook, she protested, "Oh no, don't. You'll change and I'm afraid we won't be friends anymore." Luckily that didn't happen. They stayed friends. It isn't impossible. Friends of Brookies sometimes defend them by saying they are "Christian, but not crazy like those others."

As with other evangelicals whose stories I've told, Susan and Mark Bruk's faith is bolstered by signs and messages from God that may come daily and by a community that affirms those perceptions while also providing the kind of tangible support other Americans can hardly dream of. Elmbrook members brought meals to the Bruk family for months, cared for their children, cleaned their house, gave them presents ranging from gift cards for fast food to a pricey Lenox nativity scene.

At one low point, when Susan and other church members heard that Mark needed a second surgery because of a hole in his stomach, they were in the waiting room in a circle, praising God. An African-American woman with a Bible in her hand approached them and said, "God is with you. He has not abandoned you, and he is limitless in his power."

Although Susan and her friends had spent so many hours in the waiting room that they knew everyone there, they had never seen the woman until that moment. They believe they hadn't seen her because she hadn't been there.

"We believe she was an angel sent by God to encourage us. I believe it more strongly today than I did then. I believe that God wanted us to continue to live with hope—even in the face of death. That is the power of the cross and the resurrection," Susan wrote me in an e-mail.

Elmbrook Church's annual Christmas gathering for women gets a good crowd from our neighborhood, but I'd declined invitations each of the two years before. Such massive Christmas programs are common recruiting tools for evangelical megachurches, which present them as their gift to the community. Some years, one of Elmbrook's gifts to the community is an authentic Bethlehem village that costs one hundred thousand dollars to construct. I'd seen similar high-dollar reconstructions in Texas when I was a religion reporter for the *Dallas Morning News*. Twenty-six-thousand-member Prestonwood Baptist Church, in Plano, Texas, gives a Christmas play with fifteen hundred cast and crew members, three camels, a calf, a horse, a donkey, five sheep, and a lamb. Six flying angels wearing twelve-foot gowns descend from six stories high. The choir and orchestra have six hundred performers. "Even Broadway can't match the scale of this church holiday pageant," enthused the *Dallas Morning News*. Seventy thousand people a year attend performances.

The year that I first saw Susan Bruk, part of Elmbrook's gift to the community was thousands of big iced Christmas cookies that women of the church must have spent weeks baking. Home-baked cookies have a friendly midwestern touch that I liked. It was marred only a little by admonitions that required the women to take only one cookie and not carry any home. Understandable, though: even a megachurch couldn't bake for everyone's family.

As we've seen at Lake Pointe with Van Grubbs's benevolence, successful evangelical churches never lose sight of their main purpose: making converts and bringing them into service for God. Megachurches such as Wisconsin's Elmbrook and Texas's Lake Pointe can't afford to—literally. They are enormous businesses with million-dollar budgets based on voluntary giving. Many finance their building programs with loans so big they would have scared an old-fashioned preacher speechless. Most have mission statements, just as businesses do, and they quote them often. No matter what the modern megachurch is sponsoring, the purpose is the same—bringing 'em in and signing 'em up for Jesus. It's God, God, God, all channels, all the time. Where are you with God? What are you doing for God? What does God want you to be doing?

Susan Bruk's Christian singing trio, called Sacrifice of Praise, was part of the Christmas program the year I was there. After the group sang a few songs, she told her story. She didn't overdramatize it, didn't play it for tears, but her pain was so raw that every woman there must have felt a chill. I did. To have three small children when your husband died was like something from a hundred years ago. Things like that didn't happen anymore. Not in prosperous, healthy Brookfield, Wisconsin. After talking about how terribly she missed her young husband, who had seemed so solid and indestructible, Susan said how much she wished he were alive again. Then she said that if she could have him back alive, but in return she would have to give up Jesus, she would choose Jesus. Everyone gasped, or maybe it was only me.

Two friends sat with me. One was a former member of Elmbrook Church; the other was a lifelong Catholic. The evangelical friend smiled sadly and whispered a few details of Susan's story. The Catholic looked as stunned as I did. I repeated Susan's story many times in the next weeks. It was often greeted with silence, and then maybe one noncommittal word like "Well." One friend asked, "Why even go there?" Another friend said, "Oh, I get it. It's that martyrdom thing they teach them to do."

And, of course, that must have been part of it. It would have to be in a religion founded on martyrdom. Cynics might also note Susan's audience. To have said, "I'd trade God, Jesus, and the Holy Ghost to have my husband back" would most likely have ended Susan's appearances on the evangelical circuit and needlessly weakened the faith of a community she loves. Further, cynics might note that Susan's choice is a dramatic way of showing faith but not exactly a Sophie's choice—from the title of William Styron's famous novel that tells the story of a Jewish mother being forced by Nazis to choose which child will live and which will die. Susan won't get her husband back, no matter what she chooses. Jesus is all she has left.

Lest you think me too brutal in the face of such sorrow, I ought to point out that Susan, a clear thinker despite how her story might be interpreted, understands her position quite well. When we talked, she mentioned having had a choice as her life began to spiral into sorrow: trust that God is in control and all will be well, or fall into despair. Quite apart from any action or lack of action on God's part, Susan's decision was rational. Or desperate—call it what you will. She was about to drown. God threw her a rope. She grabbed it.

"I wouldn't have made it without God," she told me.

Any psychologist, even one who thought the whole God thing was hooey, would have to affirm her coping strategy. Shrinks call it reframing. It's powerful stuff. Don't sell her short by thinking that Susan denies her pain, or that she pontificates with pride. When I met her a few years after Mark's death, she said repeatedly, "I'm not trying to act like I don't have any problems." She has spent many days sobbing. She is still lonely.

"When Mark was alive, I knew what it was like to be loved," she wrote me in an e-mail. "He was so kind and caring. I have to tell you, though, that I feel more loved by God today than I ever did before. God's love has been so real to me. God has been over the top, amazing."

Whether her perceptions are correct or not, whether her God exists or not, might be debated; what cannot be denied is that her faith has spun the straw of a young widow's sad survival into the purest, most incorruptible gold. At the end of her e-mail message she wrote, "I just want you to know how crazy God is about you. There is no one He made that is quite like you. You are so unique and very, very gifted."

She signed off with "Praying that you will know the blessings of God as I have."

In the nicest way possible, Susan was letting me know that I could have the relationship with God that she has. It was not a pitch for conversion, unless her whole life is one—which of course it is. Her words were an honest good wish, an offer to share her treasure, an assurance that God offers the same triumphant life to everyone who wants it. Would I want to know the blessings of God as she has? Sure.

But the odds are against me. Susan has flourished in a place that strangled me. Perhaps she is more obedient; certainly she is more devout. She gave more of herself to God; maybe he gave more of himself to her. I am not like Susan at all and never will be.

But that isn't the case with all evangelicals. In fact, I'm a lot more like the majority of people who call themselves evangelicals than Susan is. They say they've accepted Jesus as their savior, just as I did, but they don't have Susan's kind of faith. They don't have her attitudes. They don't have her behavior. When we talk about that 25 percent of people who tell pollsters they are evangelicals, 18 percent of them are closer to the rest of us than they are to Susan Bruk. Those evangelicals are the topic of the next chapter.

End of chpt. 5

Chpt.
Six ⟩ goes to pg. 95

SINNERS ONE AND ALL

Susan Bruk and Van Grubbs are front-runners in the faith marathon. They and other front-runners—sleek, fast, strong spiritual strivers—get all the attention. They are the 7 percent. Behind them come the mass of evangelicals, the rest of the 25 percent who call themselves evangelicals, the piddlers, the amblers, the habitual stumblers, those who stroll, and those who take long breaks from faith. They believe they were saved by Jesus and that Christians like them are the only ones going to heaven. They believe that the Bible is the word of God. If asked whether Jesus is important in their lives, they say, "Sure." What kind of person wouldn't say Jesus was important? That would only add to the rest of their sins. Many in this great mass of evangelicals resemble Ashley Smith far more than Susan Bruk.

Remember Ashley Smith, the woman who used evangelical megachurch pastor Rick Warren's *The Purpose-Driven Life* to convince accused rapist Brian Nichols to turn himself in? Ashley was held hostage by Brian, who had escaped from custody and allegedly killed four people. She shared parts of the book with him, talked about how it had changed her. This man who had murdered other humans was so moved that when she told him she needed to go pick up her little girl at a church function, he let her go. What a story. What a warm glow. What a triumph for the evangelical way.

And then, as Paul Harvey likes to put it, there's the rest of the story. Right before Ashley shared those tips that meant so much to Brian, she gave him a hit of crystal meth. Ashley winced as she heard Brian snorting a noseful of meth crystals in the other room, because she knew how they burned, and she prayed. She was praying that God would help her and vowing that this time she would turn her life around. Now, I'm not trying to pick on Ashley. She was truthful about herself, which is more than many people are. I'm merely saying that most evangelicals are pretty much regular folks, in attitudes and deeds. They do lots of things they shouldn't do and have attitudes their preachers wouldn't approve of. They aren't set apart from the rest of the country in nearly the ways evangelical leaders would like us to think they are.

In fact, misbehavior is so widespread among the great mass of those who call themselves evangelicals that evangelical author Ronald Sider calls the statistics devastating.[1] When pollster George Barna looked at seventy moral behaviors, he didn't find any difference between the actions of those who were born-again Christians and those who weren't. His studies and other indicators show that divorce among born-agains is as common as, or more common than, among other groups. A study by another group showed evangelical men no more or less likely to beat their wives than other men, while another showed that wives in traditional, male-dominated marriages were 300 percent more likely to be beaten than wives in egalitarian marriages.

Popular evangelical speaker Josh McDowell says evangelical kids are only 10 percent less likely to engage in premarital sex, and some scholars say that's too high a number. Of the more than 2.5 million young people who signed the Southern Baptist abstinence pledge, True Love Waits, surveys showed that only 12 percent kept their promise by their own admission.[2] Another study showed that some of those who were claiming virginity had gone on record the year before their pledge as having already lost that attribute. The number of evangelicals who've had sex outside marriage is so large that some evangelicals now talk about ways to reclaim your virginity through repentance, a good spiritual idea but physically unlikely. Mark Regnerus, a professor of sociology at the University of Texas, found that evangelical teens lose their virginity slightly younger (16.3 years of age) than mainline Protestant and Catholic teens (16.7 years of age) and are much more likely (13.7 percent) to have three or more sexual partners by age seventeen than mainline teens (8.9 percent). There was one bright spot in the abstinence efforts. Kids who signed the pledge didn't have sex quite as soon as they would have without the pledge, according to one study. They waited eighteen months longer on average.[3]

Waiting rooms of abortion clinics are also full of evangelicals despite the efforts of four thousand crisis pregnancy centers, often supported by evangelical churches. The crisis pregnancy centers aren't losing the fight because they fail to employ any weapon at hand. Women at such centers are frequently told that abortion will increase their risk of breast cancer, infertility, and "post abortion syndrome"—assertions contrary to overwhelming scientific research, according to a recent Congressional study. Even with such scares, evangelicals make up one out of every five women who get abortions.

At Dallas's oldest abortion clinic, Routh Street Women's Clinic, a longtime manager estimates that evangelicals make up more of their clients than anyone else. Why? Dallas has more evangelicals than anything else. When *New York Times* reporter John Leland went to a Little Rock abortion clinic to talk with women getting abortions, he found that evangelical Christians were plentiful. Some were coming in for their second or third abortion. They were repenting just as fervently as they did the other times. Some evangelical women proclaim the holiness of their faith's standards right through their second and third abortions, and take the blame every time. They're sinners who promise not to sin again.

Why should evangelical women at abortion clinics surprise us? Everybody is having sex—married, unmarried, in between marriages—just as they always have. It's a human trait. By the age of forty-four, 99 percent of people have had sex and 95 percent of them have had sex before marriage, according to the highly respected Guttmacher Institute. Those figures have remained virtually unchanged since the 1950s, according to the institute, which might lead one to wonder if evangelicals have always been kidding themselves about their faith's ability to curtail sex, or it might lead us to think that evangelicals aren't at all who we think they are.

Perhaps both surmises are true.

Christians and other religious people have always been subject to charges of hypocrisy. Nonbelievers have always said that evangelicals don't behave better and sometimes behave worse than everyone else, but now they have the statistics to prove it. Evangelicals have reacted by generally admitting their failures even before they've failed. Every time I brought up hypocrisy and many times when I didn't, evangelicals rushed to confess that they are sinners who talk the talk better than they walk the walk. "Hang around long enough and you'll see me be a hypocrite," a Bible teacher, sometime missionary, and Christian father told me. He can't help it. It's a fallen world, evangelicals say. The church is a hospital for sinners, they say. Just because we don't live the standards doesn't mean the standards aren't good, they say. Don't look at us, look at Jesus. Good advice. But not all the sins of evangelicals are the result of weakness. Some result from what David Kinnaman and Gabe Lyons, the authors of *UnChristian*, call "major cracks in their moral perspectives."[4] Among evangelicals aged twenty-three to forty-one, 59 percent believe it's all right to live with someone they aren't married to, 32 percent think having an abortion is permissible, 58 percent have no trouble with gambling, and sex outside marriage seems fine to 44 percent.

It's important to also understand that evangelicals view matters of sin quite differently than many people in today's society. If an evangelical has an abortion, takes drugs, or sleeps with someone she's not married to, she does not bring tales of it to church. Certainly she doesn't want the church people to know what she's doing, but she also may not tell her story because if she did tell it she would be required to repent and foreswear such behavior immediately. If she wasn't willing to repent, she might very well be counted as a double sinner: bad enough to do it and bold enough to tell it. Shameless.

Perhaps evangelical attitudes in this regard are more misunderstood than they once were because of a shift in American culture that seems to have taken hold in the 1960s. People began to worry about authenticity. Caring about what others thought of one's behavior was deemed cowardly. The failure to flaunt was falsification that might result in deep psychological damage. These attitudes are a long way from evangelical thinking, which is that doing wrong and then calling it right or even making it public, as if demanding that others agree, only makes you a bigger wrongdoer and a fool as well. If an evangelical is gay or living with her boyfriend, the least she can do is make sure her parents don't know it. Admitting it would be throwing it in their faces, a deliberate affront and disrespectful challenge to their values.

So how many true evangelicals, like Van Grubbs and the Bruks, like those committed, certain, unswerving Christians we've been led to believe populate America so thickly, really exist? We've looked at the most basic measure of evangelicals—involvement in church—and we've found only 7 percent instead of 25 percent. We've looked at the moral issues so important to evangelicals, and we've found that the majority of people who call themselves evangelicals aren't living up to those standards by any measure, their own included. They're behaving just like the rest of us, and in some cases they're behaving more badly than the rest of us.

But that's not enough. If the 25 percent of people who say they are evangelicals don't go to evangelical churches and don't live by evangelical standards, we might excuse them by saying that humans are weak and sinful creatures. So let's add another measure. Let's look at what this large number of evangelicals actually does believe. If they don't believe like evangelicals and they aren't behaving like evangelicals, are they really evangelicals? No. They aren't, not in the way that most of us conceive of evangelicals today. They can't be. Being an evangelical is all about behavior and belief. So let's examine what people who call themselves evangelicals believe.

The person who has looked most closely at what these self-identified evangelicals believe is pollster George Barna. What did he find? He found the same thing that I found when I looked into church membership. True evangelicals of the kind that most Americans are talking about when they use the term *evangelical* are 7, sometimes he says 8, percent of the population and dropping—down from 12 percent in 1991. To understand how he discovered this, we're going to have to delve into what exactly defines an evangelical. This is at the heart of how America came to be so deceived. Two different definitions are being used. Two different groups of people are being counted as one.

Before evangelicals came to be such a powerful political force, definitions didn't much matter. Everything about evangelical doctrine was pretty much insider baseball because not much was at stake for the rest of society. Nobody cared or had a reason to. But once they gained power, the idea that evangelicals numbered one out of four Americans and that being an evangelical meant that you supported a religious-right agenda to change society gave them enormous clout. They were believed to have big numbers and firm, unyielding, monolithic opinions. Anyone who said they represented this group would have a seat at the political table, perhaps at the head of it, and would have been looked to by the media as a spokesperson for vast numbers of Americans. If religious-right evangelicals had been seen as the well-organized but overpublicized small special-interest group that they actually are, they would never have been able to dominate the national discourse as they have.

The fact that two different definitions are being used also explains why 25 percent of Americans say they are evangelicals when only 7 percent actually fit the common perception of what an evangelical is. What Barna found is that when people and pollsters say 25 percent of Americans are evangelicals, they are using a definition that many people don't understand because it's hardly ever spelled out. It is the same definition that many pollsters, reporters, and academics use—the same definition I started with. They are talking about people who have confessed their sins, accepted Jesus as their savior, and believe they are going to heaven because of it—people who are born again. I could fit in this category if I wanted to count myself in it, and on certain days if a pollster caught me in the right mood, I might.

But when the word *evangelical* began to be used in the larger society by the press, the politicians, and leaders of the religious right, all sorts of attributes got tagged onto it. Nobody ever spelled that out. Nobody seemed to realize what was happening. I didn't. Other reporters didn't. Maybe even evangelical leaders didn't. But George Barna, an evangelical who definitely fits within our committed 7 percent, did.

He realized that we were talking about two different groups that both had the right to call themselves evangelicals. One group, the 7 percent group that we've been talking about in the stories of Van Grubbs and the Bruks, was the truly committed, religious-right group. It was a subset of the larger group. The other, larger group comprised evangelicals who were born again but didn't accept the great majority of the most basic religious tenets that evangelicals are "supposed" to live by. They held a wide range of ideas and opinions and didn't accept nearly all of the religious tenets that people associated with the religious right and conservative evangelicals adhere to.

Everybody knew this group was out there. Jimmy Carter is an evangelical who isn't in the religious right. Al Gore is an evangelical who isn't in the religious right. Bill Clinton is an evangelical who isn't in the religious right. A big percentage of Baptists who don't go along with the Southern Baptist Convention are evangelicals who are not in the religious right. But the media and the public at large seemed to take little note of the fact that these evangelicals might count for anything. The religious right, with the media following right along, branded them as liberal or progressive evangelicals, often despite their protests that they, too, were conservative. Their religious views were either ignored, disparaged, or seen to represent such a small group that they didn't matter. When in fact they—Gore, Clinton, and Carter— may be more like most of the people calling themselves evangelicals than the religious right is. At least in terms of religious beliefs. Let me spell out what I mean by talking more about how Barna did his research.

Barna didn't ask people to say what they call themselves or what they think they are. He didn't give them a list of choices, such as evangelical, Catholic, or Protestant. He didn't ask one or two belief questions and let it go. Instead he has nine criteria of belief and commitment for true evangelicals. These nine criteria identify the kind of evangelicals most of us think of when we say *evangelical*. Here they are:

1. They believe they will go to heaven because they have confessed their sins and accepted Jesus as their savior.

2. They have made a personal commitment to Jesus that is still important to them.

3. Their commitment to Jesus is very important in their life today.

4. They have a personal responsibility to share their religious beliefs about Christ with non-Christians.

5. They believe that Satan exists.

6. They believe that eternal salvation is possible only through grace, not works.

7. They believe that Jesus Christ lived a sinless life on earth.

8. They believe that the Bible is accurate in all that it teaches.

9. They believe that God is an all-knowing, all-powerful, perfect deity who created the universe and still rules it today.

Barna developed the nine criteria using a definition used by the National Association of Evangelicals. He counted everyone who agreed with all nine statements as an evangelical. Anyone who didn't agree with all nine, he said, was not an evangelical.

That didn't mean that they weren't born-again Christians. If they agreed with the first two statements, they were saved by Jesus, but they weren't evangelicals in the way that Barna and the rest of America understands evangelicals. Everyone who agreed with the first two criteria (they were saved and going to heaven because they'd confessed their sins, and they had a personal relationship with Jesus that was important to them) was clearly a born-again Christian. And that's what Barna called them. He found that not 25 percent but 38 percent of Americans met the two criteria.

Then he took everyone else who also agreed with the other seven statements and said they made up a different group. This group constituted the true evangelicals. Barna found basically the same groups that we see in church statistics: a small number I've called the front-runners—committed, true evangelicals, people like Susan Bruk and Van Grubbs—who make up 7 percent of the population; and a great big mass of other people with varying beliefs and behavior, who number at least 18 percent if you use self-identification polls and 31 percent if you use Barna's figures.

From my days as a Southern Baptist, I'd say Barna's nine criteria are a straightforward list without a lot of sticking points. Most of the really controversial stuff isn't in there. There's nothing about Jesus being God, about his bodily resurrection, his virgin birth, his second coming, or his death as the sacrifice and atonement for human sin, which are all standard fare for most evangelicals and for most Americans. There's nothing in there about Jesus being the only way to salvation. Barna's definition lets in loads of folks who wouldn't pass a doctrinal test in local evangelical churches. Even so, and this is an important point in understanding evangelicals of today, it has been so controversial within evangelical circles that Barna's credibility has been threatened among his fellow believers. Their gripe? Barna's definition of an evangelical is too exacting. As one lifelong Baptist told me, "St. Peter himself won't set that high a test."

After hearing that, I read back over Barna's definition of an evangelical. The only remotely controversial part would be the total accuracy of the Bible's teachings, but I know plenty of non-evangelicals who would say yes to that without giving it another thought. The same could be said of the idea that Satan exists or that Jesus didn't sin. Barna's nine questions are not an exacting measure at all. Any Baptist schoolkid would ace that test. In highly evangelical parts of the country such as the South and the Midwest, the great majority would claim all those beliefs, either because it would make them seem like good people or because it would keep the evangelicals from targeting them or even because it's just good manners to do so. Why start a fight with your neighbors when you don't have to? And remember, people aren't stewing over these questions. They aren't sitting across the table from a bunch of scientists. They're answering over the phone, with one ear open for what's happening on TV, and giving the fastest, least controversial answers possible. They aren't allowed to quibble or qualify or think it through. Maybe they think the Bible is totally accurate in all it teaches; maybe they haven't really thought much about it and "totally accurate" seems OK or like it ought to be true or might be true. If God's listening, he certainly won't take offense if they agree. So they say yes.

If Barna's measure is controversial among evangelicals, it must be because many of them don't hold these beliefs and still consider themselves evangelicals in good standing, which points out how greatly we've been deceived by popular portrayals of evangelicals. Those portrayals were so persuasive that even I was deceived, and I knew better. I'll give you an example. During the last Southern Baptist convention held in Dallas, I was a religion reporter. That was the year that the convention voted to boycott Disney for its anti-Christian, anti-family direction. Knowing Baptists as I do, I decided to go on the convention floor after the vote to ask the delegates what they would do and what their congregations would do.

To understand what had just happened, it's important to understand that the Southern Baptists are a loose confederation of churches. Each church is independent. The representatives are called messengers, not delegates, and don't represent the churches. Some may be questioned about how they will vote, but they represent themselves alone. They are generally the more conservative members of given congregations because those are the only Southern Baptists who want to go to the convention. A lot of other church members just want to be left out of all the wrangling that takes up so much of convention time. Southern

Baptist surveys show that only a small minority of evangelicals even know the names of the leaders who are supposed to be leading them politically, the leaders who are so often quoted by the media as representing them. Whatever the messengers at a Southern Baptist convention decide is not the will of the churches; it is merely a representation of what that group believed on that day. It does not bind anyone. It is merely a resolution, a statement of opinion, a suggestion that churches may or may not follow. That in itself, which is rarely explained in news stories, shows us that the power of the convention is often overrated. The lack of true representational power is even more pronounced at the National Association of Evangelicals, where a board decides policy and delegates aren't even used.

So after the Disney vote in Dallas, I went on the convention floor to ask messengers if they had voted for the boycott. If they had, I asked whether their churches would go along with the boycott. Most of those who had voted for the boycott laughed and said they wouldn't place any bets on that. Others said, flatly, no. When Southern Baptist kids started crying to go to a Disney movie or to visit Disney, the very delegates who voted to boycott were pretty sure the kids would win the adults over. Some of them said that they wouldn't obey the boycott themselves. They had voted on it as a way of making a statement. Many didn't think Disney had transgressed so terribly, but they wanted that symbol of American innocence to know they valued its image and wanted it to stay untainted. Their good humor and their basic good sense were a long way from the heated rhetoric of their leaders and from the media image they have.

Those convention-floor interviews showed a side of the Baptists I remembered from my childhood. Many were reasonable, thoughtful, devout, and measured. They had those qualities when I agreed with them, and they had those qualities when I disagreed with them. A lot of them were open-minded enough that they could and would talk about anything. Squelching debate or taking over America was nothing they had the slightest interest in doing. My convention-floor interviews among the most conservative, political, and devout of Southern Baptists and Barna's survey showing two groups—born-agains and true evangelicals—both show the diversity that exists within evangelical ranks. His surveys and my convention-floor coverage shoot all sorts of holes in the idea that evangelicals are a monolithic, unthinking, unreasoning, unstoppable force, which brings us to an important point about the evangelical outcry over Barna's definition of evangelicals. His test requires that the respondent answer yes to all nine of the questions. That's not unreasonable, and certainly his evangelical group gives us the best count of the kind of evangelicals we see dominating the national discussion of values. But many evangelicals do find Barna's nine qualifications unreasonable because getting a yes to all nine requires too much conformity of belief.

Barna wasn't content to merely survey the general population. He also wanted to know how the denominations stacked up. So he surveyed them. Remember once again that these surveys aren't done by visiting churches. They're done on the phone. Barna has a strict test for who will or won't be counted as an evangelical, the nine criteria, but he has no such test for denominations. People merely say which denomination they consider themselves members of. So what we have reflected in the following numbers is how many true evangelicals there are among people who *say* they belong to certain denominations. Barna found only three denominations where at least one-quarter of adherents qualify as evangelicals: the Assemblies of God (33 percent), nondenominational Protestant (29 percent), and Pentecostal (27 percent). One out of every seven Baptists (14 percent) met the evangelical classification. So what does that mean? There are three possibilities.

- The first possibility is that evangelical churches are doing a terrible job convincing their own people that essential truths of their faith are believable, in which case the people inside evangelical churches aren't who we think they are.

- The second possibility is that true evangelical church members are giving the correct answers but vast numbers of people who aren't really church members are *claiming* to be, in which case the number of people who say they are members of evangelical churches is vastly inflated.

- The third possibility is that both are true: people who aren't church members are saying they are, and at the same time people who really are church members don't agree with their leaders on big parts of doctrine, in which case the number of evangelical church members is vastly inflated and the number of true, conforming evangelicals within the church is vastly inflated, too.

The third possibility is the most extreme, but as we look at our next set of evangelical beliefs, it will seem more and more likely. The idea that all evangelicals hold the same moral values is simply not true. When the Pew Research Center for the People and the Press asked American evangelicals to self-identify without using Barna's nine questions, it found surprising attitudes among those who considered themselves evangelicals. The majority of white American evangelicals, 58 percent, do not believe that school boards should have the right to fire gay teachers, and an even greater majority, 62 percent, reject the idea that AIDS might be a punishment for sin.[5] Other surveys show that 25 percent don't think homosexuality is wrong, 27 percent don't think having an abortion is wrong, 32 percent don't think smoking marijuana is wrong, and 40 percent don't think sex between unmarried people is wrong. Only 20 percent of evangelicals consider themselves part of the Religious Right.[6] And sometimes evangelicals are even further left than the rest of the country. For instance, evangelicals are slightly more likely to believe that astrology impacts one's life (13.6 percent) than Americans as a whole (12.3 percent).

Once again, let me recap what we know so far before we move on. Salvation still changes lives. Evangelical faith still delivers all it promises. Even so, evangelical churches aren't baptizing nearly enough people to keep up with population growth, and baptisms are falling. Among the white middle class that's been their political, economic, and social base, they rarely make a true adult convert. The great majority of people being baptized in evangelical churches are already baptized Christians and children. If we judge the number of evangelicals in America by beliefs and commitment or by real numbers inside the churches, we find that evangelicals aren't one out of four Americans, or 25 percent, but one out of fourteen, or 7 percent. No city in America has a percentage of believing evangelicals as high as one out of four.

The one-in-four number comes from self-identification by a less committed, less believing, less motivated group that one evangelical pollster calls born-agains. They may number as high as 38 percent of the population, but that number means almost nothing in real terms. Their ideas, their behavior, and their religious notions are far closer to those of the American mainstream than to those of true evangelicals. The Republicans can't count on them. The preachers can't count on them. And truly conservative evangelicals wouldn't dream of counting on them.

The upshot of all this is that evangelicals number 15 million adults, a large enough group to make a difference but in percentage terms a tiny proportion of Americans, and they are not growing enough to make a difference. Nonreligious people, whose numbers are rising, outnumbered them two to one in 2001.

We have been duped. Evangelical power is based not on large numbers but on two other attributes. The first is hot air wafted about by a compliant media, politicians who gain by exaggerating such numbers, and religious leaders interested in increasing their own power. The second attribute is organization. Even 7 percent of the population, if it is well organized, focused, cohesive, and has uniform beliefs, can be enough to deliver a national election.

Evangelicals can send politicians of both parties scurrying. They can skew the national debate. They can claim moral rectitude as their exclusive property. But they are not representative of the American people. When politicians bow to evangelical will, they are serving a small special-interest group, not a large percent of their constituency. That is becoming truer every day as the United States becomes less Christian and less formally religious. Evangelical power inside the Republican Party has been formidable. Outside the Republican Party it is mostly puffery, which explains a political mystery that has long puzzled observers and angered evangelicals. Why haven't evangelicals gotten more of their agenda passed on the national level?

Election after election, evangelicals turn out, get credit for delivering the election, and then feel betrayed when candidates don't give them what they promised. They've been working against abortion for thirty years, and it's still legal. They've been working against gay marriage rights forever, and they haven't gotten any momentum for the constitutional amendment they want. They're now working against hate-crime legislation and probably won't get their way on that. Their national legislation victories are mostly bones thrown their way in alleys where the public isn't likely to look. For instance, they get faith-based-initiative money. That's nice and helps build the Republican evangelical voter base, especially among African-American churches that get money. But so what? There's no great outcry about that because there's no large group that's getting hurt by it. Their other major victory has been barring recipients of foreign aid from supporting abortion rights or the use of condoms.

Most Americans don't even know that's happening, and if they do, it doesn't affect their lives one bit. Pretty wimpy victories for a movement that can make or break presidents, but not at all bad for a small, organized, committed, media-savvy, and loud part of the population.

So now we're ready to move on to the second phase of our examination. They aren't big, they aren't growing, but are they really in for a fall? Can they make a comeback? No. In the next two sections, we'll look at dangers from inside the evangelical church and dangers outside it that are dealing mortal wounds to a faith already in distress. In each case, we'll see the paradox we started with being played out again: the appearance of great strength and success masking weaknesses that are quietly bleeding the faith and promise to hasten its demise.

End of chpt.6

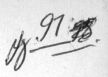

Part Two

THREATS INSIDE THE EVANGELICAL CHURCH

Chpt.
Seven) goes to pg. 115

GIANTS CRASHING

The recurring motif in this story of America's evangelical power is the classic stuff of literature and life, a theme that is illustrated nowhere better than in holy Scripture. It's the story of Moses, who, even as he led the chosen people, overstepped his authority and was not allowed to cross to the land chosen for them. It's the story of Saul, who obeyed his own fears and consulted the witch of Endore instead of trusting the Lord. It's the story of David, whose desire for Bathsheba caused him to have her husband killed. In all of Scripture only Jesus resisted every temptation and left this life unsullied.

It might not be too much to say that any time in human life when power, wealth, and prestige accumulate to mighty heights, a fall is in the making—which brings us to the story of the evangelicals' greatest triumph and impending failure, the great American megachurch. These supersized churches, which report two thousand to thirty-six thousand in average attendance, numbered more than twelve hundred at last count. Many are far more conservative than the Southern Baptists I grew up with, more educated, richer, more easily mobilized to change society, and far more focused. They are citadels led by people who brilliantly bolster the attitudes and opinions that support the most conservative kind of evangelicalism, the kind that frightens other Americans the most.

These churches deliver excellence in everything they do. Mind-blowing, constant, innovative excellence melded with an approach to the Bible that's pulpit-banging conservative, unswerving, never changing, a bold drumbeat well maintained and ever present, presented by a God in control of everything. A first mistake outsiders make about conservative evangelicals is to believe that they don't understand modern times. The smart, focused men leading the evangelical movement's most successful churches often understand what's going on before the rest of us do. Their ability to respond to the needs and desires of people caught during a time of rapid, disconcerting change is awe inspiring. At first look, modern megachurches seem impregnable, giants that awe unbelievers, causing their hearts to be afraid. They are veritable Goliaths. But as you read of their power, recall that the great majority of their triumphs are built on the same shaky foundations we've been looking at. They also have troubles all their own. Ones they never publicize. We'll look at their virtues first and then their "vices" or weaknesses.

The megachurches' reach goes far beyond their purported weekly attendance of 4 million. They say they have between 8 million and 12 million participants, and they indisputably have plenty of sway outside their congregations. In 2005, four megachurch pastors' works were on the *New York Times* bestseller list. One of those books, *The Purpose-Driven Life,* by Rick Warren, pastor of Saddleback Church, is the bestselling nonfiction book of all time. Megachurch ambitions are unbounded in scope. Their Bible-based, business-savvy approach is being franchised into mini-denominations of ultraconservative Christianity. The in-place to be in many communities, megachurches have better gyms, better ball fields, better skate parks, better sound systems, better childcare, better entertainment, better auditoriums, and sometimes better schools than anything the community can supply. Critics call them country clubs for the sanctified, citadels for Jesus, big-box churches, Wal-Marts of religion selling "Jesus lite."

Megachurchers laugh, kindly. They can afford laughter and anything else they want. They can bring Randy Travis in for a concert, stage a Christmas play that rivals anything on Broadway, keep so many children in the nursery that the infants have to be bar-coded as they check in, park so many cars each Sunday that amusement parks train their parking staff. Lakewood Church, which bought the Houston Rockets basketball stadium and turned it into a church, brings in more than a million dollars a week in offerings, compared with the typical American church, which operates on a hundred thousand dollars a year. Dallas's twenty-eight-thousand-person Potter's House produced a Grammy-winning record. Houston's twelve-thousand-person Brentwood Baptist has its own McDonald's. Arizona's Radiant Church spends more than sixteen thousand dollars a year on Krispy Kreme donuts.

Megas, built on young families, never forget the children. At California's twenty-two-thousand-person Saddleback, a children's play area has three crosses atop a Golgotha-like hill and a stream that can be parted like the Red Sea. Twenty-seven-thousand-member Prestonwood Baptist in Plano, Texas, has eight playing fields, six gyms, and sixteen thousand people on its athletic teams. At Seacoast Church in Mt. Pleasant, South Carolina, kids are slimed or whip-creamed and play air guitars at church as part of the entertainment. Once a month at a special kids' service called KidStuff, parents and kids team up to play Nickelodeon-style games with lots of yelling and lots of mess. The twenty-five-hundred-person Life Church in Edmond, Oklahoma, gives kids life-size animatronic characters to interact with, a garden, a jungle, an under-the-sea area, an ark, and a three-dimensional Toon Town.

Megachurches are cloning like mad. NorthWood Church in Keller, Texas, with two thousand–plus members, has started one hundred daughter churches with more than twenty thousand participants. Showing churches how to grow and franchise themselves is a million-dollar business. Willow Creek Community Church in South Barrington, Illinois, earned $17 million in 2004, partly by selling marketing and management advice to 10,500 member churches from ninety denominations, according to *Business Week*. Lake Pointe Church's Pastor Steve made regular pilgrimages to Willow Creek as a young man. Now, like hundreds of other big-church pastors, he sells his own expertise, helping smaller churches learn how to launch capital campaigns for multi-million-dollar buildings.

Megachurches turned to business gurus such as the fabled Peter Drucker to teach them the ways of big-business success. One of the techniques they perfected was marketing. A big lesson came from Willow Creek founding pastor Bill Hybels, who went door-to-door surveying consumer likes and dislikes about church. He wanted to know why his target consumer group, young families, weren't "buying" church. One common answer was: men. Families weren't going to church even when women wanted to because men weren't willing. He theorized that if a church could engage men, women and children would follow. It's the same lesson that television and movie producers learned at about the same time. All three products have been shaped accordingly. For megachurches and aspiring megachurches, that has often meant increasing sports and war language, always popular among evangelicals. At North Carolina's Englewood Baptist Church, for instance, a celebration of God and country included parachute jumps into the church's ball fields by a Green Beret parachuting team, some of the best-trained killers in the world.

At Saddleback, spiritual growth is compared to a baseball game, with each step forward called a base. At Lake Pointe, Pastor Steve's most common metaphor for the church is a football game. He likes to tell his flock that some people sit in the stands watching while others play on the field. His job is to get everyone playing. Lake Pointe does not allow women to teach or to lead men. Church leaders pondered the matter five years before deciding that the biblical way wouldn't allow it. A number of Lake Pointe members told me that the rules also have a practical result. Men are forced to the forefront, encouraged to take over jobs that they would otherwise leave up to women.

These megachurches' allegiance to a modern business model also means that they borrow money in larger amounts than churches of the past, thrive by continually improving their product, and survive by expanding their market. Product branding is important. The Rock in Evergreen, Washington, owns a Super Stock car with its name plastered on it and a rodeo bull chute. Every time a cowboy rides out of that chute the announcer calls the church's name. Marketing is also key. The new complex for Crossroads Church in Corona, California, was designed using Disney World ideas. It will be marketed not as a church but as an entertainment and shopping destination called Candlewalk. The complex, called a campus in megachurch speech, will anchor shops and nine restaurants. Stage I, the church's auditorium, was designed to bring big-name entertainers to Corona. It opened with Lodestone (a popular British rock band) and Olivia Newton-John.

Product development and quality control are also vital. Rockwall's Lake Pointe writes its own adult Bible-study curriculum, which it sells at $275 for a three-month package. Two hundred fifty churches use it. Each lesson "has H, B, L, T," said Carter Shotwell, executive pastor of ministries, who writes the lessons. The letters stand for Hook—grabbing the attention of the learner, Book—getting into God's Word, Look—at your life, and Took—what is the take-home. All classrooms have televisions and DVD players for music, video clips, and PowerPoint presentations.

Megachurch magic isn't confined to the United States. The biggest, most vibrant ones in the world are outside American boundaries. South Korea claims the largest in the world with 1 million members. Megachurches in the developing world are so successful that megachurch pastor Bob Roberts of Keller, Texas, doesn't even study what's happening in the United States anymore. He takes his lessons from the even bigger churches overseas. What they're doing and what U.S. megas are doing dovetails so nicely that if you want to see what twenty-first-century Christianity is going to look like, head for Asia or South America. The rise in extravagant supernatural action that's growing in churches here—healings, daily signs from a personal God, speaking in tongues, demon possession—is in full bloom there.

When I was first looking for a church to focus on, I picked Steve Stroope and his ten-thousand-person Southern Baptist church in Rockwall, Texas, partially because the church is Southern Baptist, although it doesn't use *Baptist* in its name. I also picked Lake Pointe because I liked Pastor Steve. To understand megachurches, you ought to like the front man. Suspect his motives, bridle at his manner, and you're out of step from the very start. He's the guy who draws the crowds and keeps 'em happy.

Pastor Steve built Lake Pointe Church, which started in 1979 with seven families meeting in a bait house at the edge of nearby Lake Ray Hubbard. Excuse me. God built the church into an enterprise with a twelve-million-dollar-a-year budget, with a five-thousand-person auditorium on thirty-four acres, and "Steve helped," one of his faithful congregation reminded me gently.

Steve Stroope could be the poster boy for an American megachurch pastor. Compactly built, handsome, and perfectly groomed, Stroope is so ironed and properly turned out that it's hard to imagine him ever getting mussed. In Texas such men are fairly rare and often elicit a short description: "He's the kind of guy who creases his blue jeans." Stroope may not, but you get the point. He's not cool enough to be sloppy, not hip enough to city ways that he doesn't still value a good, sharp crease just like his daddy did. And most important, he's perfectly attuned to his place and time, as are other megapastors. Californian Rick Warren wears Hawaiian shirts. Houston's Joel Osteen wears a white-toothed smile.

Pastor Steve, like his counterparts, also enjoys being in control and admits it freely. When he travels, for instance, he is always the driver of any car that's used. His staff members don't even walk toward the driver's seat. They know whose seat that is. At work, he's exacting on himself and everyone around him. A pastor CEO with all the requisite business books on his shelves, he likes taking a gift book to appointments. Depending on the issue, he might give away business guru Marcus Buckingham one day and expositor/pastor Warren Wiersbe the next. His assistant, who says of herself that she's willing to do anything for him that's not immoral or illegal, keeps his calendar so completely that she even schedules date nights for him and his wife and makes sure that Thursday nights are open so he can be with his grandchildren. Date nights are a relatively new addition to a married evangelical's obligations.

When I asked Pastor Steve how many hours a week he works, he shrugged and said, "How many do you work?"

I laughed and said, "Who knows?"

"He tries to be a regular guy," one of his church members told me once, "but he can't quite do it." Too organized, too smart, too private. "He could have done anything, been the head of some large corporation, but instead he's serving God," another church member said.

Stroope's church is located in an outlying, fast-growing, well-off suburb. A large reason megachurches grow is because of where they usually locate—in burgeoning suburbs. Young families, attracted to the suburbs' less-expensive housing, want religion for their children. They're energetic, and they have rising incomes. Megachurches have enormous overhead and a huge need for volunteers. Burned-out megachurch staff members sometimes complain that they spend more time "feeding the beast" than feeding the flock. Feeding the megachurch beast requires a constant hunt for "good" families. To the dismay of the more idealistic, good families don't mean those who need God the most but those who are committed, able, energetic, and prosperous.

In order to keep growing, megachurch pastors work to stay ahead of the curve. When the auditorium is 80 percent full and the parking lot is 90 percent full, for instance, a planner needs to start adding more space. Visitors won't come back to a church that doesn't seem to have room for them. Even members will drift away as the hassle factor rises with the crowds.

Megachurches are the great success story of evangelical Christianity.

But as great as the megachurches are, they aren't invulnerable. In fact, say many insiders, not only are they vulnerable; they are destined to fail. For years I've been hearing that they won't last, and for years they've just gotten bigger. And then one night, talking to a church consultant, I heard once again that megachurches would soon be in trouble and I said, "Prove it to me. I hear it, but nobody is convincing."

So he did. One after another, he laid out the factors that are causing so many insiders to predict that the megas will turn into minis sooner than most of us can imagine.

First, there's the problem of the pastors. Most churches have been built up by one baby boomer pastor who combines great pulpit skills and an easy, friendly manner with superior business and management ability. These pastors have an excellent sense of what progress-oriented, power-motivated boomers want. The great majority of the pastors are nearing retirement age. When they go, the consultant said, they can't be replaced. Seminaries aren't training enough people to replace them, and their congregations won't follow new, younger men. In fact, in the handful of megachurches where the pastor has retired or died, times have been tough. When W. A. Criswell, the legendary pastor of First Baptist Dallas, stepped down from the top leadership post in 1991, the church began a slump that hasn't turned around yet. First Baptist is now on its fourth pastor and $11 million in debt. Membership has dropped from twenty-five thousand to ten thousand.

Some First Baptist troubles have been attributed to its urban location—the central business district of Dallas. But that kind of trouble may soon hit megachurches also. The suburbs that gave megachurches their growth are filling up and growing older just as suburbs closer to cities did. These giant churches may find themselves in the same situation as the inner-city churches, saddled with million-dollar facilities that they can't merely jettison for a move to greener pastures.

Insiders are predicting that Ted Haggard's fourteen-thousand-person New Life Church in Colorado Springs probably won't survive his resignation after he was accused of hiring a male prostitute and resigned. As I write, he has been gone less than a year and the church already has lost almost a third of its congregation. At Elmbrook, the Wisconsin church near my former neighborhood, the founding pastor only recently retired, but rumblings of discontent have already begun. Other megachurches that have lost their founding pastors are following First Baptist Dallas by keeping each new pastor only a short time before losing him and being forced to go on to a new one—a scenario for disaster.

Megachurches may be especially vulnerable to changes in leadership because of the makeup of their congregations. Attendance, not membership, is the yardstick they use for success. This shift was one of the modern megachurch's brilliant innovations. It sets up a two-tier system, with members and attendees having fairly and sometimes completely equal status.

Some megachurches make membership more difficult than traditional churches, requiring that people not only accept Jesus and be baptized but also go to training classes, write and give personal testimonies, pledge that they will join Bible studies, give money, and witness to a certain number of people. As a result, those who join tend to be more committed than members in less demanding churches, according to theory. That gives the megachurches a sturdy, hardworking core. At the same time, low-pressure tactics and congregations big enough for anonymity bring in visitors who feel free to come back often without feeling they have to make commitments. They can attend any of the church's functions and use any of its services just as if they were members, and no one looks askance. Some churches—Lake Pointe, for example—even have rolls for regular attendees.

Other successful megachurches don't concentrate on membership at all. In fact, so many focus only on attendance that when the Hartford Institute for Religion Research did its latest survey of megachurches, researchers eliminated the question about membership altogether. They asked only about attendance. They found that 30 percent of those people megachurches count in their attendance figures are marginally committed to the church and 10 percent are merely casual return visitors. Since they attend infrequently and may also attend other churches, their total number might be 80 to 100 percent higher than the number counted each Sunday. Megachurches get little money or time from these people, but they increase the excitement level that comes with a big crowd; they also increase the church's profile by identifying themselves in the community as members of the church. This large crowd may include especially high numbers of people who don't fit the clean-cut profile of evangelicals, because megachurches generally offer many twelve-step recovery programs. Megachurches also offer a good home for the minimally committed, because senior pastors tailor their messages to a large crowd. At Lake Pointe, for instance, a number of people mentioned that Pastor Steve Stroope's sermons are uplifting and informative without being too doctrinaire, but that pastors and teachers at other levels in the church seemed more aggressively fundamentalist. One longtime Baptist couple was attracted enough by Pastor Steve's sermons to attend an adult Bible fellowship class, where the teacher railed about Russia's plans to invade Israel to such a degree that they felt as though they had dropped back into the Cold War. They didn't return to Lake Pointe. If they had stayed among the large crowd of marginally committed members who only attend main services, their feelings might never have been ruffled. They might have felt quite comfortable attending for years, never knowing about the church's most conservative beliefs.

As an example, I know one Rockwall family that did attend Lake Pointe for years without joining. The wife was a Methodist; the husband was an atheist. He liked the upbeat messages of Steve Stroope's sermons and the church's low-pressure methods enough to keep attending, but neither he nor his wife was interested in joining smaller groups. They were initially drawn to the church by their teenage boys, who liked the activities. At one point a committed Lake Pointe couple befriended them.

When they realized the husband was not a believer, the Lake Pointe couple began to pray for him and invited the Methodist/atheist couple to dinner. During the dinner the Lake Pointe members began witnessing to the husband, who reacted so negatively that the dinner broke up, and now when either of the couples spots one another in public, they veer off in separate directions. Nevertheless, the Methodist/atheist couple might still be attending Lake Pointe if a youth leader hadn't mentioned that the band Metallica was an instrument of Satan. The older of the sons, a fan of Metallica, refused to go back to church, and the family followed him out of Lake Pointe just as easily as it had followed him in.

This slightly committed 40 percent of megachurch participants means that commitment from a large part of the church is low, centered mainly around the senior pastor's appeal and around services within the church that they don't usually pay for. Faced with the loss of that pastor or any decline in the church's consumer appeal, they may quickly go back to sleeping in on Sunday morning. That high number of marginally committed members isn't the only unique danger that megachurches face if they lose their founding leader. They also are vulnerable at the other end of the participant spectrum.

The Hartford Institute's Scott Thumma found that megachurches have a highly dedicated core of 5 percent who are church leaders and an added 15 percent who are committed to a great degree. These two groups are heavily involved many hours each week and give great amounts of money, but for the megachurch many more volunteers and much more money are needed. "Few megachurches would survive, although there are some that try, with just 20 percent of participants involved," Thumma writes. They desperately need the next 40 percent of attendees who are weekly worshippers, solid participants, and financially committed enough to give 5 to 10 percent of their incomes.

Megachurches could also be more vulnerable than traditional, denominationally affiliated churches because they are so often nondenominational or downplay their denominational ties. Their emphasis on being Bible based means that they can attract highly committed Christians who want a church that hews closely to conservative, literalist interpretations of Scripture. Their allegiance to the church remains only as long as the church continues to teach lessons that match their own reading of the Bible. If a new pastor were to seem to deviate, their loyalty isn't to a denomination with family ties through generations but to the Bible, and they would leave without compunction.

Megachurches are also endangered by the market-driven methods that have caused them to prosper. Like any such business they are vulnerable when the market changes, and it may be changing. Many of the baby buster or Gen X generation and those behind it, which would include everyone born after 1965, don't appear to be as interested in big, splashy, entertainment-driven churches. There's some controversy about whether they actually are deserting the big churches in particular. According to many observers, however, this group is more likely to want smaller, more intimate settings where they can form close relationships. Perhaps even more chilling are studies that show that when they do attend megachurches, busters and those behind them don't give as much money as the boomers. The Consumer Expenditure Survey of 2004 shows that donations to religious institutions range from 0.75 percent to 0.79 percent of after-tax income for Americans aged twenty-five to forty-four. The percentage jumps two-tenths of a percentage point to 0.99 percent as we move into boomer ranks, those aged forty-five to fifty-four, and goes steadily upward to 2.38 percent for those over seventy-five. Evangelicals are accustomed to getting 4.43 percent of their members' income, a number that has dropped from 6.7 percent in 1968 and seems destined to drop even more as younger generations take over.[1]

For all their faults, boomers are high-energy, socially minded big consumers, and they are happy to splash their money in many directions. They'll put up big funds to sponsor a big show. They like comfort, achievement, and status. They'll do whatever it takes to be at the head of the pack. Megachurches, with their consumer-focused, progress-oriented approach, give hard-charging baby boomers just what they like to get for their money. They've ponied up big bucks to build elaborate facilities and sponsor the most high-tech extravaganzas. The best of everything is just barely enough for the boomers.

But those who've come after them have a different orientation to spirituality. They're more low-key—community oriented, but in a less aggressive way. All the flash and dash of baby boomer culture strikes them as shallow and inauthentic. They like smaller, more intimate settings and fewer but closer friends. Baby boomers work the crowd; busters turn away from it. They suspect anything that seems too proud of itself. They don't let go of their money as quickly as boomers do, and when they do, they don't give as much of it. Elaborate shows of religious status don't loosen their purse strings. Several young people who had grown up in big churches and left them told me that all they see when they look at a megachurch is a rich church that doesn't need their money. They didn't build those buildings, and they don't want to pay to keep them going.[2]

These younger generations want the money they do give to go more directly to programs that benefit the poor and help people who need it. Big buildings, big parking lots, massive programs, elaborate marketing, a church so big it has to bar-code children to keep up with them—all of it seems excessive and wasteful to them. As Christians, they feel they have a different calling. So they give a little to the church and the rest elsewhere—to smaller programs that they think make a difference.

This trend may account for the rapid increase in charitable projects among megachurches, which seem to have exploded in recent years. When I began covering evangelical churches more than a decade ago, the biggest conservative evangelical churches weren't known for being excessively concerned about the needs of the poor. They might do a school-supplies drive, give away some groceries at the holidays, and maybe have a giveaway room filled with members' cast-off clothing. Fifteen years ago, Texas's Prestonwood Baptist, which was about to build new facilities that would total more than $100 million, had a few volunteers and one African-American pastor as staff for the church's most consistent outreach to poor communities. They bused kids from nearby apartment buildings and scraped around for the money to open an after-school counseling center. Trying to get volunteers to help them was always a problem. Now Prestonwood Baptist has an entire warehouse equipped for loading big-haul trucks to take away all the goods it gives to the poor. The predominately white church recently partnered with a Dallas African-American megachurch for a citywide benevolence effort.

Lake Pointe seems to have followed the same path. After admitting to his congregation that he hadn't cared as much about the poor as he should have, Lake Pointe Church's Pastor Steve Stroope said the Lord led him to see that the church should be doing more for the unfortunate. Lake Pointe is now building a park and constructing a community center in one of Rockwall's poorest neighborhoods. The center will house health clinics, tutoring, Bible study, and Christian clubs for children.

This new evangelical largesse among megachurches isn't focused just in the United States. Evangelical churches are adopting villages, countries—even whole continents, as in the case of Rick Warren's twenty-two-thousand-person Saddleback. His focus on AIDS in Africa and the millions of dollars he's directing there might be the best chance that continent has to seize our attention and finally excite some concern. Lake Pointe Church sends volunteers to and supports churches in Cuba, Africa, Mexico, and Russia. NorthWood Church in Keller has "adopted" the country of Vietnam, helping orphanages, hospitals, universities, and microbusinesses. When I told North-Wood's pastor that I'd noticed a huge increase in evangelical churches' outreach to those in need, he replied that congregations won't support a church that isn't concerned about hunger and want. That's a statement that would never have been made twenty years ago. These efforts could make the megachurches more attractive to younger people, but at the same time the churches are going at them in their usual big baby-boomerish way, which means they're putting loads of money, expertise, and volunteer time into these missions.

This brings us to another danger for megachurches. Amid leadership changes, money and volunteer flow are likely to decrease, and even a short-term slump could have more dramatic and quicker consequences. Megachurches, run on a business model, thrive like any business—by expanding and improving before the product seems outdated or worn. Their niche marketing strategy causes them to be heavy on services for members, which means they must have huge budgets to keep the pace. Their building programs, their missions, their children's programs, their worship services—all have to be top rate, which requires top-rate staff and plenty of volunteers. At Willow Creek the children's programming alone requires a thousand volunteers a week. As quickly as megachurches burn out one family, they need to replace it. Add to their troubles the fact that their growth has been supported by location. They started in rapidly growing, young communities. As young families are priced out of communities served by megachurches, they'll move farther out, and the megachurches, pinned down by big-box facilities, won't be able to follow.

Lake Pointe may be encountering that problem. Last year, for the first time, attendance didn't increase at the main campus. Stroope says road construction was the cause, but other Rockwall residents scoff at that. The construction is minor, far less problematic than past road construction near the church, they say. They believe Lake Pointe has simply run out of nearby residents who want its kind of religion. That brings us to our last serious problem: the typical megachurch debt load. The megachurch business model requires that big facilities be built before they can be paid for. Many megas have heavy debt loads that rest on continued growth. The debt goes with their market-driven strategy. Traditionally, churches have been cautious organizations. They raise the money, and then they spend it. Worn carpets, rutted parking lots, and sound systems that screech are part of traditional churches' humble visage, but megachurches don't operate that way. They are full-service excellence seven days a week. That usually means lavish facilities—the bigger the better. During one megachurch's capital fund drive, when members of the congregation protested that it would be better to have the money in hand before beginning a project that would cost tens of millions of dollars, the preacher responded that God was calling them to be bold, to reach out in faith, to trust him more than they ever had. And so they did, and now they have a 140-acre church campus with athletic facilities, a school, and an elaborate food court. But what happens when the man who led them to build so much retires or dies? Churches that expand too quickly can find themselves with huge debt loads, high overhead, and no leader to rally them together.

All of that means that the megas are far more vulnerable than they look. Their leaders say that the churches aren't dependent on their leadership, that they grow through the efforts of small groups (at Lake Pointe they're the adult Bible fellowships) that bring in new members. That is largely true. Most people who come to the megachurches, according to Thumma and Dave Travis's research, are invited by members or regular attendees, but the super personalities, easy manner, and rare preaching ability of the senior pastors are crucial as a way of easing these visitors into the fold. When high overhead, big debt, changing demographics, and lower giving from a younger congregation are combined, the loss of a beloved and able pastor begins to seem less like a stumble and more like cause for a fall. Retirements of the super pastors are already beginning, and the big-giving, hardworking boomers are going to be going home to Jesus before too long. Those losses are already crippling debt-laden megachurches, and evangelical faith is taking a big hit.

End of chpt. 7

116-

chpt
Eight ⟩ goes to pg. 122

SCATTERING OF THE FAITHFUL

The second inside threat to evangelical faith in America is also one that looks like a strength to some. A new, fast-growing group of committed evangelicals, exactly that core group of 20 percent that megachurches rely so much on, wants deeper commitment to a faith that transcends church walls. They want to live their faith in everything they do. They're bringing it into business and recreation. They're seeking the best books on faith and following the most exciting leaders. With the ease of travel and the speed of the Internet, they have greater and greater access to more and more resources and to people like themselves. With so many options for spiritual growth, they could soon be leaving the institutional church behind. Some are forming house churches or participating in Internet churches. But others have a new option, weaving together their own churches of the individual. They do that by attending independent Bible studies, joining groups that sponsor short-term mission trips, participating in Christian business groups, gathering with workshop leaders for intense weekend experiences, and participating in Internet groups of like-minded people. Sometimes they stay in these groups for a long time; sometimes they participate for a short time and move on. Their spiritual lives are developed through a highly fluid mixture of activities and relationships that may penetrate their everyday lives. They get their primary spiritual experience through activities, through relationships, and through media. They may not attend church and feel no need for it.

Evangelical pollster George Barna himself is among these committed evangelicals, whom he calls revolutionaries. His research estimates that as many as 20 million deeply committed evangelicals are people whose primary commitment to God and the Bible is pulling them out of the establishment church. He believes that losing them will cause a large number of Christian churches to wither away. Today 70 percent of Americans get their primary spiritual experience from church. By 2025, his projections show, only 30 to 35 percent will look to the local church. Everyone else will put together ad hoc, individualized spiritual lives based on media and on a variety of groups. His book on that theme, *Revolution,* was a bestseller, though many critics say he's exaggerating the threat to the establishment.

But Southern Baptist research backs him up. "About 6 million people meet weekly with a small group and never or rarely go to church," says Ed Stetzer, director of the Center for Missional Research at the North American Mission Board. "There is a significant movement happening." An SBC study found that 24.5 percent of Americans now say their primary form of spiritual nourishment is meeting with a group of twenty people or fewer every week.[1] In addition, Barna supplies numbers showing that fewer than one out of five Americans firmly believes that a congregational church is critically important in spiritual growth. Only 17 percent believe that faith is meant to be developed mainly by involvement in a local church.

Let me give some context for how threatening these ideas are. Evangelical Christians refer to the church as the body of Christ. They sometimes call it the bride of Christ and frequently quote the biblical commandment that husbands love their wives as Christ loves the church. Believing that faith can be developed mainly outside the church is practically heresy. Christianity is inseparable from the church. What Barna is describing and himself supporting pulls the two asunder.

That one of the most prominent evangelicals in America would say the country's most devout evangelicals are giving up on church, and are right to do so, legitimizes leaving the established church. While others have talked of changing the church or re-forming it, Barna says 20 million are being led by God to turn away from it altogether. Being an evangelical and being a Christian are so intertwined that the first question one evangelical asks another is almost always "What church do you go to?" If you don't go to church, you aren't an evangelical in good standing. Now Barna is saying that virtually all of these Christians who meet his nine-point definition of an evangelical are leaving churches behind.

He argues that evangelical Christianity will be stronger than ever as the revolutionaries move to venues other than the traditional church. He thinks these fast-track evangelicals will be freed up to respond to God's calling as they never have been before. He believes they will revolutionize evangelical faith by freeing it and moving their lives into greater alignment with God's will. For Barna, as for many evangelicals, being in alignment with God's will means embracing more conservative, traditional interpretations of the Gospel.

Maybe. But smaller groups can also be more easily led in other directions by charismatic leaders with new ideas. The smaller the group, the easier it is for it to innovate and then mutate. Instead of a supporting a big church that can do big things, these revolutionaries come in and out of little groups doing their own thing. The groups are poorly structured, inadequately led, and lack any strategic framework or purpose, Barna writes. But, he asserts, those weaknesses only show that these groups are growing through God's hand. Maybe. But molding participants' opinions, keeping their doctrines uniform, and motivating them for big projects or political causes will be harder than it was before.

I attended a weekday prayer meeting that is the kind of group Barna is talking about. It was a lunch-hour gathering in one of Dallas's most affluent suburbs. People parked along the street, the door was unlocked, and people filed past the hostess's elaborately furnished living room into a large family room filled with lines of folding chairs. Hymns were playing on a sound system and people were hugging each other as they entered, while those in the chairs were praying or meditating. The service was mostly music, testimonials, requests for prayer, and something I'd never seen before in a Christian setting.

The hostess went to the front of the room and told some stories about how God was working in her life, and then she invited a group of other people to come forward and give messages to the crowd from God. Sometimes their messages were generalized prophecies or pep talks; sometimes they were specific messages for individuals. It was a cross between Pentecostalism and Spiritualism that no Pentecostal or evangelical or Spiritualist church I've ever been to would countenance. In Spiritualism the messages are given by spirits of people who've died or by "higher" spirits or spirit guides. In this case the messages were from God himself, but they were delivered through people whom God had given them to. I knew some of the people there, and they weren't orthodox believers at all. They were dedicated to God all right, but they were also dedicated to fashioning their own brands of highly individualized Christianity. America's biggest evangelical churches have flourished through strong central authority and unyielding doctrine. That has been the foundation for evangelical growth for at least the last twenty-five years. What Barna is talking about would set all those Christians free to pursue God in a multitude of unsupervised ways.

If Barna is correct about this trend, churches will lose their most dedicated believers. These hard-working big givers will leave churches without the resources they need to flourish. The great gathering of all ages and many neighborhoods, of people with a range of occupations and various income levels, that an established church can foster will no longer be supported by its strongest members. The wealth of the churches, their land and buildings and established funds for missions, will begin to decline. Young preachers will find their career options shrinking. They will have to function as independent small-business operators, creating their own religious programs. The mentoring system that churches have for young pastors will be largely gone. Each leader will be forced to find his own way, tailoring his own message as God leads him, with his own group. The open door that allowed the curious to wander into a church for a look will be closed. Anyone who wants to be a Christian will have to join a smaller group, with more commitment and fewer casual drop-bys.

The revolutionary leaders will be passionate, but not as skilled at managing voluntary groups as pastors generally are. Cliques will form. Relatives and longtime friends will dominate the gatherings. Many of them will flourish for a while and then languish. Others will split off. While they may do a lot of good on their own, they will no longer have set meeting places, regular times, cleared space that is owned in common. These groups may quickly attract converts. As Purdue sociologist Dan Olson's research shows, smaller religious groups do tend to have high rates of joining, but just as they quickly attract new members, they also quickly lose members.[2]

Barna points out that through the revolution he sees coming, evangelical values and ideas will begin to permeate believers' everyday lives in deeper and more apparent ways. That could happen. But the privatization of evangelical belief will also certainly be part of the result. No one will speak for any large group. No one will be able to claim unity of belief or behavior or aspiration for more than a handful of people. Spiritually speaking, that could be a good thing. But for the impact of evangelicals in the public square and on society as a whole, it will almost certainly mean a retreat.

As an introduction to our next chapter, let me tell you about one more study. It came from the granddaddy of megachurches, the premier model for church growth methods in the last two decades, Willow Creek. Founding pastor Bill Hybels called the results almost "unbearable" to consider. Authors of the study called it the "brutal truth."

After three years of research, Willow Creek researchers concluded that one out of four people at the church was stalled or dissatisfied with their spiritual growth and many were thinking about leaving. Who were these people? They were the church's most dedicated, its most Jesus-loving, its best tithers, and its most committed volunteers. Despite all they gave it, the church wasn't furthering their spiritual life. These were exactly the people Barna pinpointed, and Willow Creek didn't just find them in its congregation. It found the same unhappy group in six other churches across the United States.

Willow Creek pastors believe they have a solution. They must stop playing the role of parent and start playing the role of coach. Willow Creek leaders say mature Christians need to learn to feed themselves instead of relying on the church to feed them.

There is only one problem with that solution. The majority of these dissatisfied Christians are already reading their Bibles, praying, giving, witnessing, and serving. They love Jesus and their lives are centered around him. They *are* able to feed themselves. It is their church that isn't able to feed them.

And that brings us to our next chapter, where we will meet some of the many evangelicals who aren't merely thinking about leaving their churches. They've left, and sometimes they've left old-style evangelical faith as well.

End of Chpt 8

DISILLUSIONED BELIEVERS

Evangelicals' version of Christianity has been losing ground in the United States since 1900. By one measure, they have declined from 42 percent of the population to 15 percent.[1] One rough estimate shows perhaps one thousand evangelicals leaving the faith each day, most of whom leave Christianity altogether and never return.[2] As a whole, American Christians lose six thousand members a day, which is also bad news for evangelicals because, as we've seen with Southern Baptists, 40 percent of those being counted among the converted are other kinds of Christians being rebaptized. If that pool is drying up, there will be fewer consumers already sold on the product. That means a lot more unproductive cold calls to the unconverted and fewer sales to Christians who have only to be convinced that the evangelical way is a better brand of Christian faith.[3]

I was told again and again by preachers and laypeople that I needed to look at who was going out the back door if I wanted to understand what was happening to evangelical faith. That was surprisingly easy to do. It sometimes seemed as if defectors were seeking me out. Many contacted me over the Internet after reading other books I'd written in which I talked about my Christian background. Some approached me at religious gatherings. Their stories had an element that surprised me. They were being led out of conservative evangelical faith by deep spiritual convictions based on what they believed God was telling them. These committed evangelicals were becoming disillusioned as a result of their own growing relationship with God or after realizing that what the church was telling them wasn't what they truly believed. They came from the same pool of fast-track Christians that George Barna's revolutionaries were coming from, but these evangelicals were going another direction altogether—either leaving the churches or quietly beginning to disagree with the churches on critical questions of core doctrine.

I'd imagined that most believers left the church in college, as I did. I thought they left because they couldn't believe the miracles or the virgin birth or the atonement doctrine. I thought they objected to the guilt and the hypocrisy. All those things do push young people away in great numbers, but one of the great strengths of evangelical faith has been that it has retained more of its young people than other types of Christianity.

Churches of Christ have been especially good at this. They estimate that in the South, where their numbers are strongest, only 33 to 45 percent of kids who participate in church during high school drop out later. Outside their southern strongholds, however, the number of dropouts may be as high as 80 percent. And of those who leave, only 12 percent return once they've married and had children of their own.[4] Southern Baptists estimate that 88 percent of their kids leave church after high school. Josh McDowell Ministries, a group that focuses on youth, reports that 94 percent of high school graduates leave the faith within two years.[5] A crisis among young-adult believers isn't merely looming; it's full-blown. Many evangelicals say that young people have always left the church and then returned once they married and had children. That may be a shaky proposition. It's the same one that newspapers used for years. Young people also stop reading newspapers in college and young adulthood, but in the past they always started subscribing again once they got older. Then one day they didn't. The world had changed in ways we couldn't foresee, and in ways that we could have foreseen but ignored. Now newspapers all over the country are in trouble, cutting sections and laying off journalists.

Churches are experiencing somewhat the same falloff, according to Robert Wuthnow's *After the Baby Boomers.* Much of the downturn is occurring because younger generations are marrying later and having fewer children. Traditionally young people come back to faith when they marry and are especially committed when they have children. Those delays are a large, intractable reason churches aren't regaining members in a generation that's bigger than the boomer generation. Twenty-one percent of twenty-one- to forty-five-year-olds never attend religious services, compared with 14 percent of that age group in 1972–76. "The majority of younger adults either attend religious services rarely or, if they attend more than that, are hardly regular enough to be the core of any congregation," Wuthnow writes.[6]

Losing young people is an old story, but the dissenters I was meeting were of a different, even more alarming kind. They were not lightweight kids trying out different ways of being, as I had been when I left evangelical faith. These were church stalwarts whose Bibles were so well thumbed that the pages curled, midlife Christians being drawn out of evangelical faith by their own, Bible-inspired, deepest values, sometimes ones they hadn't realized they had. They were leaving evangelical faith for the same reason outsiders sometimes say they won't join the evangelicals—because they seem un-Christian. These departing evangelicals could outquote, outtestimony, outshout me anytime, anyplace. Some were leaving altogether, foreswearing the faith totally. Others were keeping their memberships intact but quietly pulling back. Some were still going to church, staying quiet but disagreeing on more and more until they could hardly be counted as evangelicals at all. Others were quietly changing their beliefs, working for a new kind of Christianity. They were breaking all the old laws they had lived by. They were committing heresy. They might be going to hell.

Their stories sounded a lot like salvation stories but in reverse. They felt a great change, an epiphany, and it set them free. A difference was that this was a spontaneous movement that concerned only them and God. There was no organized group trying to get them out of evangelical faith. They had no support. No cheerleading. Their change of heart often meant that they would lose friends, alienate relatives, and find themselves without the foundation that had ruled their lives completely. Nevertheless, they went forward.

One other characteristic of these people surprised me. They were mostly midlife women. For the evangelical church, that may be the most serious loss of all. Women are the mainstays of any religion. They're more spiritual, more faithful, more committed, more likely to give their time and energy to church, more tolerant of disappointments in church. They're the first to join, the last to defect. The three women whose stories I'm about to tell were people no one would ever have thought would buck the system.

AMY WAS AN employee of a Texas Baptist group when I met her. She was handing out a survey and giving people free books at a conference on church growth. When I told her what I was doing, she said, "You've got to hear my story." Amy and Jay, whose names have been changed, were raised in the Baptist Church, attended Baylor University, and got to know each other through Christian groups. They married, had children, and were great parents—a happy couple other people envied. Amy was on staff at a Baptist church. Jay worked for a religious charity and led the men's group in their church.

At about three o'clock one morning, Amy awoke, which was unusual, and, realizing Jay wasn't beside her, which was more unusual, went to look for him. She found him and their house-guest, a visiting Alabama preacher, in a back room of their house engaged in a moment of considerable passion. She backed away before they saw her. She can't remember how she got back to bed. God must have been holding her up. She could feel him calming her, assuring her that this wasn't her fault, that what Jay was doing with the other man came from something within him.

Even in those horrible moments, with her pulse beating so loud and fast that she thought she might have a stroke, she could feel deep within herself a calm knowing about Jay: "This is who he is." She hadn't known he was gay, never suspected, but seeing him with another man answered questions she hadn't dared ask. That night, when she felt the presence of God more strongly than ever before in her life, was the beginning of Amy's defection from evangelical belief. She was angry, hurt, betrayed, but she didn't think Jay was a sinner who could be saved from homosexuality. She knew he was a Christian. She knew he was responding to something deep within his own nature. And God, right there with her through it all, so close she could feel him in the room, wasn't telling her to believe anything different. Life knocked her down, God picked her up, and she saw with new eyes.

"When I realized that Jay wasn't who I thought he was, I began to question other things," she said. She began to be more open at church. She might say casually to the Sunday school class she taught, "I had a margarita last night, just one." As she began to open up, people began to tell her about their own problems with drinking, infidelity, with various sorts of meanness and disappointment.

Jay went to Christian counseling designed to help men who didn't want to be gay, but the deprogramming didn't work. Instead, during group counseling sessions he made new Christian friends—guys who understood exactly what he was going through. Instead of convincing him that he was a sinner, they helped convince him that he was responding to his true self. He lost his job with the religious charity, moved out of the family house, and began to be more open about his homosexuality. His evangelical parents and siblings haven't completely accepted him as he is now, but his three daughters, all devout evangelicals, have. He's still a Christian, he says, and he is living the life God made him for. He attends Cathedral of Hope, a Dallas megachurch that focuses on Christian ministry to gays and lesbians. His new partner is a former evangelical, too.

Amy refers to God as Spirit now, doesn't believe in hell, and does believe in reincarnation. She wouldn't feel guilty if she slept with her boyfriend or if she set up housekeeping with him. She refuses to say grace over a meal, and if anyone asks her to deliver a prayer aloud, she refuses. "It's just not something I want to do," she says. Her faith is stronger, she adds, and it's her own, not something someone else believes.

"I'll never back down from my beliefs," she says. "They mean too much to me."

Amy is far from alone. Let me tell you about Cathy. She was a spirit-filled, tongue-talking, holy-rolling Pentecostal who followed Jimmy Swaggart, watched the PTL Club, and hung on the words of Paul and Jan Crouch. Her four children weren't allowed to see movies, listen to rock music, or read unchristian books. Newspapers weren't allowed in her home because they contained a horoscope. If anyone had told her three years ago that she would believe as she does now, she would have said, "That's a lie of the devil. I rebuke you in the name of Jesus."

Her deconversion started when her son Adam's friend was killed in a motorcycle accident. When Cathy asked Adam if he had witnessed to his friend about Jesus, Adam replied that he didn't believe in the devil or in hell. Cathy was horrified, fearful, and then depressed that all she'd done to pass on her faith hadn't worked with the people closest to her. What exactly did that mean? She couldn't bear to think about it, but she also couldn't shake the funk it put her into. One day in the break room where she works she saw a copy of the religion section of the *Dallas Morning News.* Her eye fell on a small headline: "Preacher Under Fire for Views on Salvation." Datelined Tulsa, Oklahoma, it read:

> The Rev. Carlton Pearson, the high-profile pastor of Higher Dimensions Family Church, is under fire from fellow evangelicals for teaching that almost everyone will be saved, even those who do not accept Jesus.

Cathy should have reacted with outrage at such heresy. The old Cathy would have, but something had shifted in her when Adam so forcefully repudiated the beliefs she had taught him. In the dark days following that moment, something had opened in her, and now a new Cathy spoke up. She thought, "That's what I've believed my whole life. I've never believed people went to hell." From that moment on her evangelical/Pentecostal beliefs started to fall away. She prayed about what was happening, took her deepest fears and desires to God. She believes he answered by leading her to new ideas that her church would have cast her out for speaking aloud. Each new idea led her to another. She realized that she didn't believe a lot of things her church was teaching. Maybe she never had and she'd been too afraid to admit it. Now she had alternatives. She believed they'd come with God's blessing. As time went on, she began to form another kind of faith altogether. Eventually, she walked away from church itself.

"I'll never go back," she says. "I think Christianity is the most insane religion." She no longer believes that the Bible is literally true or that people need forgiveness from original sin.

"I'm still exploring. I think I am where God, Jesus want me to be."

Would she call herself a Christian? No.

"I am nothing. But that article set me free, so to speak. It set me on a path to freedom, to an open mind and a freedom to explore, to question. I could never have done that before. I believe we have a Creator, and I believe we should live the best life we can, for ourselves, for others."

Helen is another of those estimated one thousand people a day leaving evangelical Christianity. A thirtysomething woman from suburban Chicago, she now calls herself almost-an-atheist—a title she made up because calling herself an atheist tends to agitate evangelicals, and the last thing she wants is to be offensive to anyone. Helen's defection began during what many of her fellow Christians considered her finest hour.

Helen was participating in a Christian weight-loss program called the Weigh Down Workshop that was captivating American evangelicals and earning millions of dollars with the idea that God didn't want them to be fat and would help them lose pounds without dieting or exercise. Developed by a woman named Gwen Shamblin, the program eschewed exercise because that means focusing on the body and it eschewed dieting because that means focusing on food. The only biblical way to lose weight was to focus on God, Shamblin taught her clients. By the time Helen took the Weigh Down Workshop, Shamblin was a bestselling author and her workshop was being offered in thirty-thousand-plus churches in seventy countries.

Agog with the good news that God wanted her to be skinny, Helen hung on to Shamblin's every word and searched the diet leader's Web site for every bit of wisdom available. Along the way, she made an unhappy discovery. She realized that the program's founder didn't believe in the Trinity. That was outrageous to Helen and her fellow evangelicals, unacceptable—ungodly even. Helen publicized Shamblin's wrong doctrines among friends, put up a Web site, spread protests on the Internet, and started a national outcry. The weight-loss program began to lose business. The *Wall Street Journal* did a story on the controversy. So did *Christianity Today*. Helen was a heroine to lots of evangelicals. Pretty heady stuff for a humble little Christian in the suburbs.

And then one day Helen realized what she was doing in the name of God: She was destroying the business and the reputation of a woman with hopes and dreams and the right to speak out on her beliefs, a woman just like her. She was doing this merely because the woman had ideas that didn't correspond with hers. She realized that she wasn't acting out of love at all.

So she stopped. She shut down the Web site she had started. She apologized to Shamblin. She refused to do any more work against the Weigh Down Workshop. The Christians who had helped in the Shamblin takedown tried to talk Helen into rejoining their efforts. Some began to attack her. They said maybe her own Christianity wasn't what it ought to be. And so Helen began to get a taste of the bitter dish she had helped serve up.

She had been so certain that she was acting as God wanted her to. Her fellow evangelicals were still sure of it. But they were wrong. So what was God really saying? Was it possible to know? Like many devout evangelicals, Helen read her Bible every day. As she read, she prayed that God would speak to her. And he did. He had told her to spread the word about the diet leader. Hadn't he? And if he hadn't, how could she sure about anything she thought he was saying?

Helen began to feel that she needed a vacation from God. She told him she wasn't going to pray or tune in to him or read the Bible for a while. And here was the strangest part: she didn't miss it. For years, she had felt the palpable presence of God every day. Now he was gone. And she didn't miss him.

Then there was another strange thing: at church, nobody noticed. Her brothers and sisters in Christ, those people she had believed to be so much closer to God than she was, didn't even notice. God didn't tell them. She, who had once been of one mind and one accord with her brothers and sisters in Christ, was now sitting in their midst, an apostate practically, and nobody noticed.

She started questioning things she had never before doubted, and as she did, it was as though she had been cocooned in duct tape and now it was peeling away. She realized she didn't like the tone of the apostle Paul's writings and that the book of Matthew seemed vindictive. Contradictions in the biblical text now seemed more important. Her own views came rising up now as she read the Bible, and she realized that she hadn't been thinking her own thoughts but rather what others told her to think. She realized that she didn't really believe that people were going to hell if they didn't accept Jesus. She didn't agree that women shouldn't speak in church. She didn't really like the God in the Bible, and she couldn't really understand how anyone could love him.

She was wading steadily deeper into unbelief, and soon it began to frighten her. She had often heard Christians say how hopeless and meaningless life was without God. Was that true? If she kept thinking her own thoughts, flexing her own muscles, if she didn't bind herself up in the duct tape of unquestioning belief again, she was going to lose her faith. Would life be joyless and dead, devoid of purpose? Whom to ask? Who would know? Atheists, perhaps. She found the Internet Infidels Discussion Board and began to post on it. She peppered the site with questions and observations, out-posting everyone else by far. Most of the atheists were gentle with her, just as good and kind and caring as Christians, perhaps more so. Over days and weeks and months of conversations, she realized the atheists didn't feel bereft and without hope at all. They felt free. They could think about anything they wanted to. She wanted that.

One day she announced to the Internet Infidels Discussion Board that she no longer considered herself a Christian. She started telling her Christian friends. Some friends suggested that she join a more liberal church, but she won't. As she wrote in a recent newspaper column, "I don't want to belong to any group claiming their way to God is superior to some other group's way."

These three women of faith, these hard-chargers, these confirmed, lifelong believers, have left evangelical faith. They are only a sample of those who've done the same. They've been led by experience, by life, by their own ideas, and in two of the cases, they believe they've been led by God. The first one refused to turn against the husband she had always considered her best friend, refused to believe his homosexuality was a sin he could conquer. The second one realized she didn't believe that everyone was going to hell and that she never had. The third one followed what she thought was God's leading until it made her self-righteous, unloving, and sanctimonious. Then she quit. She stopped acting in those ways, and eventually she stopped following that God.

SO NOW WE'VE seen two kinds of defectors leaving in huge numbers, both kinds from among core members of a faith that doesn't have nearly the strength we've been led to believe it has. The first type of defectors are Barna's revolutionaries, who aren't finding what they want in established churches. The second type aren't finding what they want in evangelical faith as a whole. How many are there? Millions—not by my count, not by the count of unbelievers, but by the testimony of Christians themselves. As we've seen, one study sees six thousand Christians a day, perhaps one thousand of them evangelicals, leaving faith altogether, and another says an extra 20 million intensely committed evangelicals are on the way out of established churches.

Defectors who leave evangelical churches or faith for any reason are a serious threat. But those who leave the faith altogether as a matter of conscience undercut the faith in a way that little else could. These defectors, who know the faith's strengths and weaknesses, its rewards and punishments as no outsider ever could, are joining the outside world, agreeing now with those who disdain the most precious foundational ideas of evangelical Christianity as not only wrong, but wrong before God. The evangelical movement that is at the forefront of American's culture wars could absorb these losses if it were attracting other adults to replace those it is losing, but as we've seen, it is not. Part of the reason is the poor behavior of evangelicals themselves, which we've explored a bit already. Part of the reason is evangelical doctrine, as we've seen in this chapter. In the next section, we're going to look at evangelicals' witnessing efforts and a radical new take on God developed by two Christians. Both are hastening the fall of the evangelical church.

chpt
Ten ⟩ goes to pg. 146

SHY WITNESSES, DOORKNOB GODS, BAD POLITICS

I've said the churches aren't to blame for the lack of converts. I've shown what a great job they're doing. How much they offer believers. How well they educate Christians. How adroitly they disciple them into right thinking. As we've seen, many churches are training for evangelism. They're preaching evangelism. They're pressuring for evangelism.

And members *are* responding. They're praying. They're repenting. They're feeling guilty, cowardly, and shamed before Jesus. They're even naming names of the lost ones they will pursue. Signing pledges to do it. Re-upping every year.

There's only one thing they're not doing. They're not evangelizing, and nobody, not even Jesus, seems able to make them do it. Only half of all born-again adults do any witnessing at all in a year, and what they do they don't feel good about. Studies show that spreading the Gospel is one of the areas in which Christians "have the lowest self-esteem and the least interest in self-improvement."[1] Even evangelical publishers hesitate over a book on evangelicalism, according to one such publisher. Nobody will buy it. According to Southern Baptist figures, only 16 percent of their members witnesses regularly.

Why won't Evangelical Eddie spread the Good News? Maybe because he and his evangelical friends aren't nearly as insensitive as they're thought to be. Maybe because they're pretty nice people. "They don't want to be overly dogmatic. They don't want friends to run the other way when they walk into a room. They don't want to become judgmental or arrogant. They don't want to hurt anybody," says evangelical leader Brian McLaren. He's right. Most evangelicals would no more show up at your door with a religious tract than they would run down the street naked. It would be crude, an imposition on your sensibilities. It probably wouldn't cause you to accept Christ, and it most certainly would cause you to shun them. Preachers can shame and guilt evangelicals all they want. They can get them to sign pledges and name names, but they can't get them to act in a way they know is offensive. They don't want to be jerks for Jesus, and foisting their "truths" off on people who don't want to hear them would make them just that.

As evangelical Jim Henderson puts it, witnessing isn't normal. Only that small percentage of evangelicals who are fiercely, wildly extroverted are willing to witness regularly. And most of them will have to witness to strangers, because they aren't going to have many unsaved friends. Henderson has founded a movement to soothe the timid majority and calm down the extroverted minority by advocating what he calls "ordinary attempts," Christian witnessing through kindness and friendship. His way doesn't include formulas, a litany of Bible verses, or threats of hellfire. The idea is that if evangelicals *do* Christianity instead of trying to *tell* it, they will have more impact. McLaren and Henderson believe that if evangelicals act like normal people transformed by Jesus into kinder, more caring, more generous, more giving human beings, others will become interested in Jesus. But will they?

The bottom line for evangelical faith is that believers aren't just regular people. They're the ones going to heaven, and nobody else is. Taking that stand in a relatively homogeneous, isolated culture might not cause much discomfort, but in postmodern Western culture, where many different ideas about divinity come together on equal footing, claiming to have the only truth can be seen as arrogant and probably deluded. Evangelizing among friends, no matter how sensitively it's done, is very likely to be considered a betrayal of trust, something a lot of good evangelicals—lovers of Jesus, adherents of hellfire though they are—just aren't interested in doing.

That's exactly how Delores, a Portland resident and a conservative Christian for over twenty years, felt about her friends the martial artists. She had been surprised when she felt God leading her to hang out with a bunch of martial artists who generally didn't like Christians. What surprised her further was the strong sense she was not to try to convert anyone, just to be there and get to know them. She knew her evangelical friends might be uncomfortable, but following God's lead was more important to her. Despite some apprehension, she began attending the training sessions and workshops. In time, she was delighted to learn how much they had in common. She realized the fear she had been taught in church around the martial arts, the people who practiced them, and non-Christians in general was not necessarily based on the truth. Initially, her minister was supportive, but soon the fact that Delores would not evangelize and truly grew to love these people made him nervous, and he basically asked her to choose. For Delores and her husband, leaving their church became the unexpected and heart-wrenching result of following Jesus. They are now looking for new ways of practicing their faith, ways that are more honest, respectful of others, and much less fear based.

Despite all these problems, however, half of evangelicals say they do witness at least once each year. That's a lot of folks; even once a year would be a lot of witnessing. Of course, they may not be telling the truth. Those figures come from Southern Baptist studies. If the claims Baptists make about membership versus the reality of who is actually in church are any judge, only about a fourth of the people who say they witness really do. But even if the Baptists' claims are true, chances are they witness only in the right circumstances.

Many of those who are able to side with the angels on witnessing get the chance because their church or Sunday school has put on an outreach event that makes it easy. Evangelicals who are perfectly willing to go on mission trips and witness to foreigners, or to offer God's salvation to victims of a natural disaster, may hang back in everyday witnessing—perhaps because they realize that under normal circumstances the competition is just too fierce for words alone to make much difference. Let me explain what I mean.

The single best time to convert an adult has always been when he's down and out. He hits bottom; God steps in. Any of "the big Ds" will do it. It might be drink, it might be drugs, it might be divorce, it might be death, it might be disaster. A sinner riding high is not a sinner looking for Jesus. He's got to be knocked down so hard that he knows he can't get up on his own.

For about two thousand years, for your average Western screwup the only help available was divine. And then along came two Christian men whose souls burned with a desire to help the suffering. They were responsible for the biggest shift in Western spirituality in the last one hundred years. Their program rarely makes the headlines, and when it does, no one quite seems to understand what a radical change it has fostered. With hearts full of Christian love, they decimated traditional Judeo-Christian ideas about how God works.

They wrote "the Big Book," which became the basis for Alcoholics Anonymous and all other twelve-step programs of recovery. Millions of Americans—drunks, druggies, divorcées and divorcés, even the bereaved—have taken those programs and been healed. All to the good, of course. But twelve-step programs made one critical change in Christian ideas. They switched from God to a "Higher Power" of each person's own understanding, which doesn't necessarily mean any god anyone else has ever seen or thought of. This Higher Power, this made-up god, has healing force that had previously been reserved only for known gods. Sometimes twelve-step leaders, in trying to explain how loose this new concept is, will say, "That doorknob could be your god."

And here is the critical part: this doorknob god works wonderfully. If people have no sense of a Higher Power at all, they are often stymied in their attempts to save themselves, but if they put reliance on Something—no details needed—and then add twelve steps that are psychologically and morally sound, mostly based on treating yourself and others well, they are on their way to recovery. Make public confession part of it. Then add a group that supports the recovery. Choose a sponsor to handhold and advise. Make sure people gather frequently to share their stories—that is, testimonies. Do all those things, and you can get amazing results.

You can get deliverance. Life will change. Colors will be brighter. The air will be sweeter. Burdens will drop away. New life will begin. All this from "the program," and a Higher Power doorknob. The most insidious thing about the twelve-steps concept was that it didn't oppose anything. It helped people. It worked. And it slowly exposed people to the notion that they could get the power of God without the dogma, the doctrine, and the outdated rules. Without the church, in fact. It was a kind of mini-Reformation, cutting out yet another middleman between ordinary people and God. Only it wasn't just the pope being eliminated this time. It was the preacher and the Bible and tradition.

This didn't mean that a twelve-stepper could have complete license. The steps don't forbid sexual behavior, but they do forbid falsehood, cruelty, and unkindness to others or to oneself. They require repentance and apology for wrongdoing. When evangelicals point out that the twelve steps are based on Christian ideals, they're close, but not quite right. The twelve steps are based on Jesus's ideals—the Golden Rule in particular—paired with a personal, nonspecific Higher Power. It is the coming together of two incredibly powerful ideas.

AA founders realized that even a God with no qualities, no doctrine, no book, and no preachers could bring on enormous change because they had read the work of nineteenth-century psychologist William James, who is still considered one of the best outside observers of religious conversion and who was also one of religion's most illustrious friends among scientists at the turn of the century. Although not a believer, James was among those few scientists who might accept, for example, that our New Orleans converts, Mike and Michelle Tauzin, have been truly transformed. He would acknowledge that God could be working. At the same time, he would say that transformations such as the Tauzins' often occur naturally, without any participation by a supernatural force.

Here is James's take on moments like the Tauzins' conversion:

> Emotional occasions, especially violent ones, are extremely potent in precipitating mental rearrangements. The sudden and explosive ways in which love, jealousy, guilt, fear, remorse, or anger can seize upon one are known to everybody. Hope, happiness, security, resolve, emotions characteristic of conversion, can be equally explosive. And emotions that come in this explosive way seldom leave things as they found them.[2]

It's interesting to note in support of James's ideas that 50 percent of Americans say they've had a transforming religious or spiritual experience. Of those, 35 percent say they were not "born again," which might mean that so-called conversion experiences are more common than we might think and less religious.

William James talked of only two ways to get rid of anger, worry, fear, and despair. Either you find hope, security, and confidence in some fashion and those new emotions take over. Or you give up in exhaustion. That giving up, which Alcoholics Anonymous calls relying on a Higher Power, is, in Christian terms, surrendering to God. "So long as the egoistic worry of the sick soul guards the door, the expansive confidence of the soul of faith gains no presence," wrote James. But if the ego lapses even for a moment, the soul of faith can take possession and set things right. Once the soul of faith has acquired position, it may retain it, James wrote.

Sometimes James himself sounds like an evangelical, as he does when quoting a fellow scholar, who "seems to put his finger on the root of the matter when he says that to exercise the personal will is still to live in the region where the imperfect self is the thing most emphasized." When subconscious forces take the lead, however, they marshal the better self, which becomes a precisely focused and transforming power. What then must a person do to unleash this subconscious better force?

"He must relax," writes James's source,

> that is, he must fall back on the larger Power that makes for righteousness, which has been welling up in his own being, and let it finish in its own way the work it has begun. . . . The act of yielding . . . is giving one's self over to the new life, making it the centre of a new personality, and living, from within, the truth of it which had before been viewed objectively. . . .

Man's extremity is God's opportunity is the theological way of putting this fact of the need of self-surrender; whilst the physiological way of stating it would be, "Let one do all

in one's power, and one's nervous system will do the rest."
Both statements acknowledge the same fact.

Twelve-step programs use both those ideas to help people deal
with most of what knocks them down: divorce, death, drugs,
drink, depression. The only "big D" that twelve-step programs
don't do is disaster, which means that of all the most common
opportunities for an adult sinner to be rescued by Christianity,
only one still has no competition. Maybe all those evangelicals
who don't and won't witness aren't neglectful of their Christian
duty. Maybe, instead, they're merely realistic. Until a natural disaster comes along, their brand of salvation, rule-bound and focused on sin, is no longer the only brand available. Why pay a
higher price when a lower price will buy the same results? On
earth at least. Whether the twelve steps will get anybody into
heaven is another matter.

ALL THE INSIDER threats we've talked about so far have developed over time, and they might be called the unexpected results of innocent efforts. The last insider threat we're going to
look at is a recent one that traditional evangelicals, Southern
Baptists especially, warned against in the strongest possible
terms. Thirty years ago, when the religious right began to organize politically and the Southern Baptist Convention began to
take a rightward turn, moderate Southern Baptists opposed both
movements. They believed that the convention's authoritarian-
ism was taking soul freedom away from individual Christians.
They also believed that allying Christianity too closely with any
political party would bring shame on the name of Christ. Certainly their words have proved prophetic on the last count.
During the last years of the George W. Bush administration, op-
ponents of evangelicals watched gleefully as evangelicals, high

and low, were implicated in crimes, moral transgressions, and ethical violations across the nation.

When asked to rate eleven groups in terms of respect, non-Christians rated evangelicals tenth. Only prostitutes ranked lower. Anti-evangelical sentiment is so high that many evangelicals are suggesting they would like to drop the title *evangelical* altogether. They prefer *Bible-believers* or *creedal Christians*.

A former Texas journalist who recently went to work for a megachurch got admiration and curiosity when she told people she worked for a newspaper; now she avoids the job question because people too often ask, "Why would you want to work for a place like that?" A Wisconsin doctor who left Catholicism for a megachurch summed up a common attitude among her acquaintances and colleagues: "They think you're stupid."

I've been told a couple of times that megachurches are engaged in deliberate brainwashing. A documentary producer out of California recently told me that she had it on good authority that evangelical megachurches use music, lighting, and images to hypnotize their congregations. Don't dismiss her ideas because she's from California. That state has more megachurches than any other state in the country. Megachurches use a specific drumbeat, she said. It's a scientifically studied, strictly controlled method, she added.

"Have you ever been to a megachurch?" I asked.

"No," she said.

"I have. I wasn't hypnotized."

"Some people can't be hypnotized."

"That music with a beat that your source talked about is a rock-and-roll beat usually. Nothing mysterious about it." That ended our conversation, but it didn't convince her.

Public disdain for evangelicals has only been ratcheted up by the idea that "brainwashed" people want to take over the country and force everyone to abide by their rules. Antifundamentalism is such a strong factor among many Democratic voters that political scientists Gerald De Maio and Louis Bolce say such political antipathy hasn't been seen since the pre-Depression days of ethnic and religious fighting over immigration and prohibition.[3] One survey found that only 11 percent of all Americans identify with the religious right and only 20 percent of evangelicals do so. The surge of religiosity that affected public opinion in the 1990s is reversing, says a Pew Research Center report. The average percentage of those who believe that abortion should be illegal, for instance, dropped from 19 percent in 2004 to 15 percent in 2006, while the percentage believing it should be legal in all circumstances rose from 24 to 30 percent. Acceptance of gays and lesbians is also increasing rapidly, as is acceptance of female independence. In 1997, 28 percent strongly disagreed with the idea that women should return to traditional roles. Now 42 percent strongly disagree.[4]

"People who are not religious are finding themselves marginalized, and they think it's time they spoke up and fought back," Scott Keeter, director of survey research at the Pew Research Center in Washington, D.C., told a Canadian reporter. "There is a sense that the pendulum has swung too far."[5]

As one observer told the *Atlantic Monthly,* "When the Democrats finally shattered the Republican majority in the 2006 midterms, it was their consolidation of the *secular* vote that helped put them over the top."[6]

The fallout has been so severe that columnist Cal Thomas, a former vice president of the Moral Majority, has repeatedly urged evangelicals to leave the political stage altogether. Upon the death of Moral Majority founder Jerry Falwell, Thomas wrote that little had been accomplished politically and much lost spiritually "as many came to believe that to be a Christian meant you also must be 'converted' to the Republican Party and adopt the GOP agenda and its tactics."[7] When the Center for Reclaiming America shut its doors, he applauded, decrying "the crass pursuit of the golden ring of political power" that such organizations had fostered.[8] Referring to the 2008 presidential election, he wrote, "There are many moral and godly people in my church who I would trust with my wife, but with possibly one exception, not the country. Competence, not ideology or religiosity, should be primary in this election."[9]

David Kuo, a longtime Christian-right activist who served as President George W. Bush's deputy director of the Office of Faith-Based and Community Initiatives, talked of evangelicals having a "political obsession." Florida megachurch pastor Joel Hunter told the *Orlando Sentinel* that Barack Obama was correct in saying that faith had been hijacked by religious-right leaders who exploit what divides America. A recent survey on Beliefnet.com, a nonpartisan forum on religion and spirituality, found that four out of ten evangelical voters now favor the idea of Christians taking a two-year "fast" from politics.

POLITICS GONE BAD, midlife women leaving evangelical faith, competition from individualized twelve-step gods, and evangelicals refusing to proselytize are all small symptoms of a huge reshaping that's going on in Western perceptions about how truth is found, about the meaning of reality, about the purpose of life, about the very nature of what it is to be human. Author Phyllis Tickle says what's happening isn't a mere shift in ideas. It is an earthquake in reality.[10] This earthquake has shaken the great majority of us out of our traditional-faith homes and slammed the door behind us. We couldn't get back in even if we wanted to. Our very consciousness has changed. The quake gathered strength over time, beginning with tremors that barely knocked our knees, building to waves that rattled our teeth. It wasn't a choice we made. It was the earth beneath our feet cracking, buckling, shifting itself into new configurations, into a landscape never before seen.

That earthquake is the topic of the next section, where we'll shift our focus from the inside and begin looking at outside threats to evangelical faith. Some evangelicals, aware of the danger they're in, are expecting a New Awakening, but others are beginning to doubt that such an awakening can ever come. They are saying that only a new Reformation will save Christianity in America.

End of chpt. 10

Part Three

THREATS OUTSIDE THE EVANGELICAL CHURCH

Chpt.
Eleven) *goes to pg. 157*

DIFFERENT STORIES, DIFFERENT IDENTITIES

Pastor Steve rarely preaches a straight come-to-Jesus sermon, or, as he would put it, "presents the plan of salvation," but when he does it's a doozy. The service I saw started with praise music delivered by an orchestra, drums, and guitars as well as singers. Praise music often sounds like soft-rock love songs with all the moaning and longing intact, but instead of being about the girl, they're about Jesus, who never jilts anybody. It's a good beginning.

Then came a video presentation of Pastor Steve wandering around various scenic places, searching for paradise, which was the title of his sermon. Wearing a floppy safari hat and jacket, he was shown against backdrops of Istanbul, Kuwait, London, Switzerland, Stonehenge, Paris, and at last Rockwall, outside the church and then running down the halls to make his leap onto the stage. At one point in the video, he's standing before a blooming tree on the Tigris River in Dahuk, Iraq, when he points out that the site of the actual Garden of Eden is said to be near here. The ancient city of Nineveh, where Jonah preached, was over there, he says, gesturing in one direction, and Mount Ararat, where many people believe Noah landed the ark, is over there, he says, gesturing in another direction.

I still lived in Wisconsin then. It was February, windchill thirty below, as I watched a video of that service. I was on the sofa under a blanket. When the part about the Garden of Eden came on, I shook my head like a person with water in her ears. Did he just say the actual site where the Garden of Eden was? And then Ninevah where Jonah preached? Jonah who was swallowed by the big fish and lived to tell about it? And Noah, he who put a pair of every creature on the earth in a big boat to save them when the world was flooded?

Pastor Steve, well read, college educated, actually believes that the Garden of Eden was a place where God walked and a serpent tempted Eve to eat of the Tree of Knowledge, that Jonah was swallowed by a fish, that Noah saved all the animals. Literally. From a specific place on the earth. I had grown up with all those stories and once believed them, too, without questioning. They're something you accept if you grow up in the American South, like the idea that radio waves are in the air or the fact that electrons exist. But I was a kid then.

Hearing Pastor Steve, a modern man whom I know to be a sensible father and husband, standing in an actual place, Dahuk, Iraq, on the banks of a river with a tree blooming behind him, mention almost casually that the actual site of the Garden of Eden was said to be nearby caused me to think, "That's ridiculous. He can't believe that."

But he does.

His whole life, his big church, his even bigger denomination, the Southern Baptist Convention, the entire conservative evangelical movement, and many of the policies of the Republican Party are based on the belief that such things are literally true. That's not so odd when you consider that the entire Christian faith is based on the idea that God came to earth, died, and returned from the dead. It's a great story, shared by other ancient faiths. Its symbolic value is immense. Make it literally true and it's explosive stuff.

And it makes perfect sense if you start from the premise that they start from. Religious people and most people who call themselves spiritual start with the idea that life on earth is more than the result of random mutations. They believe that life has pattern and meaning, that it originates from a source. The source that created the universe also created the rules it runs by and can deviate from those rules at any time. There's nothing revolutionary about those ideas. Those of us who've rejected them are the revolutionaries. We're the Johnny-come-latelies who've accepted the new scientific paradigm so completely that we judge everything by it. But the evangelical position hasn't lost its power, as Pastor Steve proceeded to demonstrate.

He told about how not long ago he buried a friend, Mike, who had been burned so badly in a car accident that his features and his fingers were burned off. Mike had lived for years in that condition and had found meaning in his life because he was saved by Jesus and God dwelt with him. Now Mike is dead and in paradise. His fingers and his features are restored. But the best part of paradise is being with God, the preacher said, and we can have that right here. We may think prosperity, power, and prestige will give us paradise, but they won't. Paradise isn't a place at all; it's a relationship. A relationship with God. Receive what Christ died on the cross to give you so that you can spend eternity in paradise, the preacher said.

Then Pastor Steve launched into an old-fashioned altar call. The singers started singing and the violins came in and the drums beat and the guitars throbbed. And it got to me. Just like it used to. He made it sound so good. Having God with you all the time. Paradise right here on earth. I wanted it. Who wouldn't? But I can't have it, and neither can most of America.

We don't believe the fundamentals of evangelical faith. We can't. And we never will.

LOTS OF PEOPLE blame Nietzsche. Understandable, but Nietzsche was only the messenger. He saw the terrible divisions rending the faith of the Western world more than a hundred years ago. When he wrote that God is dead, he meant that the way humans looked at God had been destroyed by reason and science, and the old ways would never recover their power. His madman mourns the loss of God in words that evoke Shakespeare's assassination of Caesar.

> God is dead. God remains dead. And we have killed him. How shall we, murderers of all murderers, console ourselves? That which was the holiest and mightiest of all that the world has yet possessed has bled to death under our knives. Who will wipe this blood off us? With what water could we purify ourselves? What festivals of atonement, what sacred games shall we need to invent? Is not the greatness of this deed too great for us? Must we not ourselves become gods simply to be worthy of it?[1]

Nietzsche's observation was a brilliant and prescient one that has held true for most of Western society. When evangelicals display bumper stickers that say, "Nietzsche Is Dead—God," they are making a clever statement. Nietzsche is dead, and they are alive. But for how long will they remain a force in the Western world? That's a chancier matter.

When Nietzsche said that God is dead, he meant that a change in the story that gave Western life ultimate meaning had occurred, and we would never be able to go back to the state of simple faith again. For more than sixteen hundred years no story had been more important to the Western world than the story of

Jesus's life, death, and resurrection. About four hundred years ago, however, a new, compelling, and, perhaps, most important, tremendously practical story began to compete with the Christian story. This story was about the efficacy of reason and science for finding truth. Almost overnight it provided greater riches, comfort, and health, and longer life, than humans had been able to even imagine.

It employed a method so simple that anyone could use it to discover new truths about the world. Ordinary humans had never been so empowered. Exploration and invention exploded. The very nature of truth changed. Verities once handed down from God and passed on intact became mere ideas, theories—hypotheses even—that any person could speculate about and test. Truth became provable, a verifiable proposition, not a tablet of rules, not a private vision, not a dream, not a proclamation from someone in power.

As a result everyone in the Western world would begin to judge reality differently, to observe the world differently, to use their minds so differently that soon they would be unable to remember a time when religious faith seemed bolstered by the world around them rather than contradicted. The Christian story, which rested so securely on untestable truth from an invisible God, was soon challenged on every front. Almost all Christians fought this new worldview; some fought it with everything they had. Others began to adapt.

When the new movement called fundamentalism began in the American Christian community about one hundred years ago, it was a direct response to this new story. Its hallmarks were militant opposition to modernity. By modernity, I mean mostly the idea that science and reason provide the proper ways, the only legitimate ways, of looking at life. That idea has led to the plethora of other changes that are hallmarks of modernity, from challenges to biblical accounts of history to birth control to foul language in movies.

Fundamentalist Christians' militant opposition wasn't active violence, but rather a way of thinking about themselves, a sense of being under attack that employed images of perpetual battle. Christianity was an army of the righteous out to slay evil. When I was a child we memorized Bible verses, which were our swords, and reciting them for our teachers was a sword drill. This new way of looking at Christianity also centered on a strengthened policy of looking toward the Bible as true in all regards and without error. Prior to the fundamentalists' new literalist approach, American Christians were far less likely to argue over such matters.

Since then the word *fundamentalist* has come to be applied to other religions and to mean something so nasty that no one really wants to claim it, but it's a term that still describes a large part of the American evangelical community. Moderate evangelicals have always complained that they are the truly conservative ones and ought to be called *conservatives* while their more rightward leaning brethren should be rightly called *fundamentalists*. To avoid biasing the reader unduly, I have called these ultraconservative evangelicals merely *evangelicals,* while sometimes taking a cue from Barna and labeling those who are less committed to a strict litany of fundamentalist ideas *born-agains*. I've divided them into true evangelicals, who are 7 percent of the population, and other self-identified evangelicals, or born-agains, who make up the other 18 percent or more, depending on how big you think that group is. Whether this ultraconservative 7 percent are fundamentalists or not, they are certainly the legitimate descendents of them.

Fundamentalists and the conservative evangelicals who followed them realized that the basis of their big story, the Bible, was under attack, and they believed that if its critics won, Christian faith would no longer have great strength. To use a metaphor from a great story, Delilah was again snipping away at Samson's hair, and these warriors for God were not about to snooze while they and God were robbed of force. They were not deluded. As would often be true in the future, conservative evangelicals were excellent weather vanes, acutely attuned to cultural storms on their way.

Hardly anything is more important to human identity than the stories we tell about life and about ourselves. Evangelicals know this; thus the importance of testimonies in their churches. It is our stories that give us meaning. They ground us, set us free, frighten us, wound us, heal us, and enrage us. The reason for this is that stories—about what life means and about who we are in that life—make up our identity. Without identity humans are lost. It's as if we don't exist to ourselves. People will starve to death without lifting a finger against those who have food but will murder over an event that happened one hundred years ago.

The truth of that is hard to understand. How could mere stories be at the base of such horrors instead of more concrete matters such as wealth or wrongs? Contrasting those conflicts with the American Civil War can help illuminate the point. That war was as horrendous as any war could be, full of savagery and loss, but the Civil War isn't still being fought and never will be fought again, no matter how many Confederate flags are flown. Some people say the Civil War receded because America had so much land to expand into. That's a big part of it. The new unexplored land of the West gave Americans a new story to focus on, a bright future, an untrammeled vista to create completely new stories, identities that they could live in. And they did.

As Nietzsche was trying to point out—hoping to be helpful, I'm sure—humanity itself is in a similar position. For the first time in recorded history, there's an untrammeled vista available. He compared it to the expanse of the open sea, wonderful and terrifying. Science and reason have given us a place where the old ways of thinking about God don't dictate as they once did. Within this new, empty vista, humans can create new stories about who they are and what they are here to do. These stories can create new identities unbound by old notions of right and wrong, of up and down, of male and female. Nothing in the great vistas of the American West, neither rattlers nor drought, quicksand nor gunslingers, was ever as frightening as that. Or as thrilling.

Unlike post–Civil War America's vista, this new vista is cognitive and societal rather than geographical. Our physical world isn't growing larger. Thanks to transportation and communication, it's shrinking, and these new stories are colliding with the old. The force of that collision is sometimes murderous, as we know from the terrorism around the world. In this country, the collision is less violent and more political. Many people believe that conflict between the old, traditional religious ways and the new ways can be won by ultraconservative evangelicals, who will push how we do government and plan families back to the 1950s, a much more theological place with fewer rights for dissenters or individuality.

In the three decades since I left the Baptist faith in a huff, the side that I had chosen, that bigger world, was going to win more and more victories over the minds of the Western world, while the evangelicals' world was going to seem more narrow, rigid, and angry. Before long people all over the country would be asking themselves, what is it with those strange Christians who were so hardened, so obsessed with controlling other people, and so intent on discriminating against people who weren't doing them any harm? Until finally hardly anyone who wasn't an evangelical would remember that it wasn't they who had changed. It was us.

When I stopped going to church, I knew I was rejecting the teachings of my heritage. I was choosing a new identity. A rebirth, if you will. But we never really leave our old selves behind—not as individuals, not as a nation. Realizing that, I finally understand why evangelicals can so easily threaten me—

and maybe the country—so much. Their certainties attack our new identities.

Few of us sit down long enough to analyze the stories we base our lives on. Most of us absorb ideas from the culture, take some, and leave the rest without quite realizing what's happening. When outsiders think about what turns them on or off about evangelicals, they're much more likely to focus on behavior. Or intelligence. Both are used as reasons for the popular antipathy to evangelical faith and the people who practice it. That antipathy is our next outside threat.

hatred
dislike
aversion
animosity
hostility
antagonism
repugnance ...

End of chpt. 11

Twelve

DIFFERENT MORALITY IN THE HEARTLAND

Not long ago, coming back from dinner, I said to two of my Methodist friends, in defense of the über-evangelicals who sometimes seem to be invading our families and neighborhoods, "What could be better than serving the God of the universe? Is it better just to schlub along, going to work, making a buck, ferrying your children around, having no great purpose, no great assurance of anything but death? Serving almighty God in almighty ways is the evangelical way, and what's not good about that?"

"Sounds like a great deal," replied my midwestern mother-of-four friend tartly, "except you have to give up your brain for it. Not something I'm ready to do." Her sentiment was the one that most often comes up when I'm trying to convince nonevangelicals that these Christians might have something good. These critics aren't completely off base, according to instructions given Christians by Martin Luther, who began the Protestant faith. He said, "Reason is a whore, the greatest enemy faith has," and

"Faith must trample under foot all reason, sense, and understanding."

Princeton's Robert Wuthnow, who was saved as a child and now studies religion, summed up the dominant cultural feeling about evangelicals' mental capabilities well. He was writing about academia, but his observations apply to society as a whole:

> [N]o groups arouse passions and prejudices more than evangelicals and fundamentalists. . . . Because evangelicalism is not a reality that outsiders have tried seriously to understand; it is a symbol for all the fears that mainstream scholars and intellectuals worry about most. Evangelicalism is taboo because it conjures up images of crazed cult members burning books, closing their minds to rational argument, and allowing charismatic leaders to rape their intellects. In a society that values higher education as much as ours, the mind is our most cherished resource. To waste a mind is, as we say, a terrible thing. Drugs and evangelicalism stand for the same thing—the loss of a human mind.[1]

The right to unfettered thinking is as deeply embedded in our cultural shibboleths as Christian values, and every day more so. As society changes more and more quickly, our need to take in information without barriers becomes more critical. The ability to change is in direct conflict with obedience to religious tradition. Survival in modern society depends on swift adaptability. "Why would anyone want to be stuck in the past?" one of my Wisconsin neighbors said with some disgust when speaking of evangelical thought.

The need to stand on one's own is also a fiercely held belief. Another neighbor put it this way: "I want to rely on myself. I could never feel secure relying on some other power that might or might not show up." I heard that sentiment echoed many chpt. 12 (cont) 161.

times when evangelicals were being criticized. The level of passion in these discussions was surprising. Everyone perceives that something important is at stake, and for many outsiders, the way evangelicals view the world imperils that something.

Let me tell you a story from a book-club meeting in the solidly Republican, churchgoing Wisconsin neighborhood where I lived for eight years. My neighbors and I were talking about our lives in a chatty, easy way. A Catholic mother of two mentioned that her college-age daughter had asked her to record an episode of *Nip/Tuck,* a weekly television drama about plastic surgeons. Her daughter couldn't catch her favorite show that week, and Mom was happy to help her out.

"Have you seen that show?" my friend asked. Some of the group had, but I hadn't. Neither had she. One day while she was ironing, my neighbor decided to play the recording she had made. The content was so raunchy that she couldn't believe what she was seeing.

"I erased it," she said. "I'm not having that kind of thing in my house." When her younger daughter protested that the older sister was going to be upset, my friend said, "I don't care. I can't stop her from watching it, but I'm not having anything like that on my machine."

That started the usual clucking and shaking of heads that talk of televised smut and violence elicits among parents, along with stories of how they restricted their children's access and how important that was. After the stories went on for a while, I said, "OK. So we all agree that these programs are awful. We don't watch them, and we don't like what their influence is doing to children. So why don't we join the evangelicals' effort and ban such programs?"

There were no evangelicals in the room, although as I've mentioned, several megachurch evangelicals do live in that neighborhood. As far as I know, among the eight women present there was only one avowed liberal, a churchgoing Catholic, and one woman with little interest in religion for herself. Others were Christians, most likely Republicans. Everyone in the room had strong moral opinions, and no one was even remotely libertine. Still, they began shaking their heads.

"Why not keep such programs off television?" I pressed.

"Because I can change the channel," said a devout Catholic.

"Nobody is forced to watch," said a Presbyterian.

The mother who had erased the recording sent her daughters to Catholic school and keeps a strict watch over their behavior. Nevertheless, she was in agreement. Not in her house, not on her recorder. But ban it from society? No.

Does this make sense? We all agree something is harmful, but we all agree that we won't do anything to curtail it? No, it doesn't. Not in terms that any traditional evangelical can understand. Artistic license? Is that it? I don't think so. Unrestricted freedom of speech? These are midwestern suburban matrons, bedrock of the country, most of them solidly Republican. There wasn't a woman in that room who would value a snarky L.A. television producer's right to produce filth over children's welfare. My guess is that they perceive some value in freedom of expression for which it is worth setting up barriers between what children and adults can watch.

Some say Americans are victims of individualism run amok, but what's happening is more complex than that. Robert Bellah made the term *Sheilaism* famous some years ago when he and his colleagues profiled a woman named Sheila. Here's how she was quoted in their book, *Habits of the Heart*:

"I believe in God," Sheila says. "I am not a religious fanatic. I can't remember the last time I went to church. My faith has carried me a long way. It's Sheilaism. Just my own little voice." Sheila's faith has some tenets beyond belief in God, though not many. In defining what she calls "my own Sheilaism," she said: "It's just try to love yourself and be gentle with yourself. You know, I guess, take care of each other. I think God would want us to take care of each other." Like many others, Sheila would be willing to endorse few more specific points.[2]

Bellah picked up the term *Sheilaism*, which came to mean someone who was hyperindividualistic, without a real foundation for moral and ethical decisions. Bellah saw such relativistic thinking overtaking society, and he worried about its effect. But at the same time, his research showed that Americans weren't behaving as selfishly as such wishy-washy thinking might lead one to expect. They were still volunteering in the great numbers that Americans are internationally famous for. They were still generous to others. They sacrificed for their children as much as, and sometimes more than, parents of previous generations. What seemed to have changed, he said, was the language. Americans no longer had a language to talk about communal, sacrificial actions. They were caught between knowing whether to honor their own needs or those of others. They still were putting aside their comfort in favor of helping others, but without the Bible or a firm sense of exactly who God is and what he wants them to do, they didn't have handy justifications for why they weren't just doing for themselves.

What I'm seeing among my neighbors and what Bellah saw in his research is part of something that has shifted since the days when television censors wouldn't let Lucy and Ricky Ricardo sleep in the same bed. Extreme individuality is part of it, but in my knit-together, generous neighborhood I saw the same things Bellah saw across America twenty years ago. We're hardly opposed to working toward the common good; quite the contrary. Every one of my midwestern neighbors and their kids seemed to have some good cause or several that we all pitched in on each year with time or money. I live now in Pasadena, California, where people have put great effort into making my husband and me feel welcome. When we asked one couple why they were doing so much for us, the wife said, "This is how we wish we had been treated when we moved here." When I question people's motives for doing good—and I do that often, because such questions are part of my work and my interest—they usually say something similar, a variation on the Golden Rule that Jesus and other religious figures have instructed people to employ. Bellah's Sheila sounded so self-centered in her first descriptions—"just my own little voice" and "try to love yourself and be gentle with yourself"—that it was easy to miss the end of what she said: "I think God would want us to take care of each other." I believe Sheila and lots of other people are falling back on the Golden Rule ethic in place of traditional religious proscriptions because it is adaptable and highly situational. They're doing that as a reaction to real changes in a world that requires a lot of adaptation to situations humans haven't been in before.

An important dividing line between the committed evangelicals who make up 7 percent of the country and many of the rest of us is that they must hold firmly to certain truths that are not allowed to change. They must not adapt or compromise on the essential points of morality because they are bound to do God's will. Whether it serves society or not is secondary. As society has changed—birth control has become available, adults have married at older ages, divorce has become more common—the old standards of sexual abstinence, for example, have begun to seem less reasonable or necessary to many Americans. Further, many Americans have come to believe that if you have a standard that great numbers of people aren't obeying and never have obeyed, it's a good idea to stop acting as though that behavior is aberrant. Failing to make that change causes more deception, which isn't a good thing. And it can cause people to act worse than they otherwise would. The great national example has been Prohibition. The stories we tell about that are of the crime that came after liquor was outlawed. The Christians who led the country to that decision are seen as misguided and fanatical. A second point—and this one is critical to the new morality being employed—is that many Americans have shifted their perception of what's right and wrong to new ground. They now say, for instance, "If nobody is getting hurt, it's OK."

Evangelical leaders spurn such ideas as weak. They call them situational ethics, with a sneer in their voices. Their assessment is once again correct: *If nobody is getting hurt, it's OK* is indeed situational, as is the Golden Rule ethic. It's flexible and workable in everyday life, impossible to achieve much of the time, but so are many moral edicts. It throws out all the rules in favor of treating your neighbor as yourself. Reliance on this kind of ethic has opened the door for acceptance of homosexuality. It has shifted the discussion about bearing children out of wedlock from an absolute wrong to a situation where marrying might conceivably be making a bad situation worse.

And it has made evangelicals, with their inflexible biblical rules, seem uncaring and, to many, unchristian. This notion of being unchristian is a bit different than the idea of being a hypocrite. Being unchristian isn't about the kind of hypocrisy that says one thing and does another. It's more serious than that, if anything could be. As people outside the evangelical camp adopt the "Don't hurt anyone" rule for themselves, they also apply it to others. Realizing that Christians were commanded to follow the Golden Rule, outsiders are less likely to understand where evangelicals, with their Bible-based morality, are coming from, and are more likely to condemn such morality as unchristian when it hurts someone by denying them certain rights or respect.

That doesn't worry evangelicals much. They're secure in knowing more about what a Christian ought to be than people who aren't even Christians. But perhaps it ought to worry them more than it does, because it hurts their witness. When outsiders see Christians behaving in ways that they consider un-Christlike, evangelicals lose the strongest impetus toward salvation that they have: their own example as the kind of person others want to be. They understand the strength of their example well, and many of them refrain from doing things they don't think are necessarily wrong—such as drinking alcohol, dancing, or card playing—merely because others might think those things are wrong. But this idea that they are mean-spirited, harsh, unloving, and unchristian when following biblical mandates is much more difficult for them to deal with. They're caught between saving their witness and doing what they think God commands. It's a dilemma that can be deadly to the Christian witness.

For instance, many evangelicals support the war in Iraq because they believe that the Bible commands them to support the president, who is in authority over them. Some believe that George W. Bush was specially anointed by God to lead America. Others believe that the United States has been led by God to fight the evil of terrorism brought by people of another faith. Still others believe that the Iraq war is a just war by God's standards. But outsiders don't parse those reasons to find understanding. They believe that the Golden Rule constrains true Christians to oppose war, especially a war as murky as this one. If evangelicals don't oppose war, then evangelicals are false Christians. Nothing these "false" Christians do can convince them otherwise.

AND NOW SCIENCE, that old nemesis of religion, is launching another broadside at the faithful, one that promises to be far more damaging than anything that came before it. Forget evolution. The new battleground is original sin. Scientific discoveries showing why humans act as they do are assaulting the moral high ground that religion has always occupied, challenging the very idea that morality and ethics are dependent on religious teachings, or are even affected by them. All those parents who come to church so their children will behave kindly and honorably are about to be told that church isn't the potent force they thought it was; that they might not even need it.

Now that researchers can measure impulses in the brain, they have proof. They know exactly what's happening as someone is tempted to act. What they've discovered is undermining the idea that humans have self-determination, an important Christian concept. They are finding that it is the body, not the brain, that may be in control. As an example, everyone is familiar with the fight-or-flight instinct. People find themselves running or bristling before their brains quite know what's happened because their senses have communicated with the body before the processing part of the brain has caught up. So we aren't running because we're afraid, we're afraid because we're running, as the saying goes.

Now scientists say that many more of our actions are controlled by the body and at lower levels of the brain below cognition. That might mean that we are not in control of our actions to nearly the degree that we like to think we are because the body reacts and then tells the brain what to do, not the other way around. We have the illusion that we're in control because everything happens so fast, but when scientists measure reactions in the body and in various parts of the brain, they can see precisely what the timing is. One psychologist says we're controlled by our unconscious, which he calls the *elephant*. Our conscious mind he calls the *rider*. The elephant moves in one direction and the rider justifies, he says. It happens so quickly that the rider has the illusion that he is directing the elephant when in fact the elephant is actually carrying a tiny, rather helpless rider wherever it pleases. The misguided rider may feel guilty or proud about the direction he is moving, but either feeling is unwarranted because he never was in control.

In addition, the body appears to store memories according to whether something was pleasurable or painful. If it was pleasurable, the body says, *Do it again*. If it was painful, the body says, *Don't repeat that*. It gives these commands mindlessly, with no intention other than pleasure. And here's the point that impinges on religious territory: the body's instinct to do what feels good and avoid what feels bad can't actually be overridden, say some scientists. Some preachers seem to realize that also. My Pentecostal aunt quoted one who told his flock, "If you haven't done it, it's only because sufficient desire has not met sufficient opportunity."

Philosophers and psychologists have debated the notion of free will forever. Psychologist William James came up with an easy demonstration of how free will operates from body as well as mind. He said that when it's cold outside, we lie in bed telling ourselves to get up, but it's cold and we don't want to. So we stay under the covers and argue the point with ourselves, but it never does any good. We don't move. And then we throw the covers back and leap from bed, but no thought precedes the motion. We realize that we're getting up only when we feel ourselves rising. The body has decided the matter before it lets the brain know what it's doing.

Science is attacking original sin on another front by questioning how morality is attained. Is moral behavior taught or is it genetic? Is it the purview of religion or is it biologically determined, a universal disposition that has been maintained and passed down genetically because humans who cooperate are those most likely to survive and pass on their genes? What that would mean in plain English is that humans are not innately sinful. Instead, they are innately cooperative or, to use more religious language, they are innately good.

As we've seen, evangelicals believe humans to be innately sinful. Goodness comes from God and God alone. Forgiveness and repentance are essential. If humans are only riders on an elephant, they don't have free will, and there can be no responsibility, no freedom to choose God or sin, no basis for hell's punishment.

If humans are "good" because the good survive to pass on their genes, then original sin becomes original goodness and salvation becomes unnecessary.

It ought to be noted that by evoking fear and guilt, religion has a counter to uninhibited pleasure seeking that serves society pretty well. Someone does something his religion tells him is immoral, and, before or after the event, he feels shame, guilt, fear of God—all emotions that the body records as unpleasant. At the same time, believers get access to forgiveness, divine succor, purpose, meaning, community—all things that increase the body's sense of safety and well-being. Religion can also tell us to avoid situations where sin is likely to occur. What all this amounts to is that Christian understandings haven't lost the battle to define human nature by any means, but attacks are once again coming from new directions where "provable" truth, not revelation, is the deciding factor.

In my research at Lake Pointe, I was struck again and again by what an excellent system traditional Christianity is for delivering both the carrot and the stick. Its benefits in socializing humans so they can live together and form healthy families are enormous. I'm not ignoring the costs and errors that religion can occasion, only saying that evangelical Christianity is a brilliant and psychologically sophisticated system. Nevertheless, if people don't have the free will to knowingly choose to do good, to seek God, to turn from sin, the central premise of evangelical Christianity—that we all have the choice to be saved—is threatened. It could be that this problem of free will, coupled with the difficulty evangelicals have in converting adults like themselves, is part of what's spurring a resurgence of Calvinism among evangelicals. If God chooses those he wants and no person is able to choose God on his own, then the scientific negation of free will isn't a problem. People aren't responding to the call for salvation because they can't. They haven't been chosen by God.

I've used scientific research as my example for a development that's changing ideas about morality because scientific ways of looking at the world are a prime mover in that regard, but they are far from the only forces molding our perceptions. We've already talked about some of the changes shaping ideas about sexuality. Multiply that a thousand times, spread it out in so many ways that we can't even comprehend what's happening, and you have what's going on for most of us every day. Economics, art, literature, mass media, the speed of change, the ease of getting information—all this is in flux constantly, and we know it. Once only philosophers knew; only the best-educated and the most intelligent people were able to perceive changes. The rest of us were clueless. We merely lived our lives, doing pretty much whatever our parents had done, and after a couple of hundred years we began to catch on that we and everyone else were thinking differently. Scholars filtered information, formed it into understandable patterns, gave good reasons for why we were changing, and then explained us to ourselves gradually, incorporating the old and the new.

They're still doing that, of course, but now we have all sorts of new information that we need to deal with, without much guidance outside ourselves. In such a diverse, thought-rich, shifting society we have to process more information and make more decisions in a day than our ancestors might make in a month, which is why evangelical Christianity with its many life-enhancing and unchanging answers ought to be flourishing. It gives solid answers to the big questions and leaves our minds free to deal with everything else. That may be why it is flourishing in developing countries. But in the West all the changes we live amid have, in the words of philosopher Richard Rorty, changed our mental software. Our consciousness has been molded into a new shape—a more skeptical, disputatious shape that doesn't yield to religious authority as it once did. Not because we don't wish to yield. But because we can't. Our consciousness is not what it used to be—an idea that evangelicals would turn purple at. To them, man is the same as he has always been, and so is God.

All these changes—technology bringing us new ideas and proximity to new kinds of people, science showing us we are not who we've always believed ourselves to be, medicine giving us new sexual options—have helped form a sense that we need to be able to act, to adapt quickly, to think on our own. We feel a visceral imperative to be more flexible than humans have been in the past, which is yet another reason nonbelievers are often angrier than they ought to be at evangelicals. Their anger seems to be deep-seated, rising out of the body, as if something is threatening them more than any cerebral argument would, as though it's their very body saying, *This way of thinking is not safe.*

As we move into the next chapter we'll see that as they raise their children, Americans are following their sense that the old ways aren't safe. Once again evangelicals have picked the right battles, the ones that define the changing pulse point of society. They've made family values the heart of their fight with modernity. So much so that the term *family values* itself is often used as a synonym for religious-right ideas. While the preachers were preaching and the political leaders were pontificating, American families were quietly going on with the business of raising children, a business that was changing quite radically.

Evangelicals saw the changes and opposed them in all the ways that they could. Skirmishes over the power of welfare agencies to investigate child abuse, over whether to spank or not spank, over what children should be allowed to read in school, and over whether prayer should be allowed in school masked much deeper core conflicts. These core conflicts dealt with new ideas about what children need to flourish, about how morality is best developed, and about what kind of adults children should grow up to be. Evangelicals sometimes won the public battles, but they were steadily losing the private ones, which they could not enter with protests or legislation or argument and which are most deeply shaping the adults of tomorrow. More than any other factor we've examined, that shaping, which begins in early childhood, is a death knell for the kind of evangelical belief we've been looking at.

End of Clyt. 12

Thirteen

chpt. 13 ⟩ goes to pg. 189

NEW FAMILY VALUES

It is in our families, the most sacred of our relationships, that we see most clearly how much evangelicals and nonevangelicals have diverged in their thinking about life. This divergence lays two different paths for how to live, for how to decide what's right and wrong, for how to respond to authority, and for how to deal with individuality. One path supports traditional, conservative evangelical faith. The other makes such faith almost impossible.

Evangelical children in the most devout households are learning to obey authority through faith and with reverence while other American children are learning that to query authority, to voice strong disagreement, to follow your own ideas, is entirely proper and right. While good evangelical parents protect their children from growing up too fast, other American parents begin preparing their children to make decisions at earlier ages. These deep-seated differences in what parents believe their children must have and in how children are being formed as a result are the greatest reasons Americans will never, and cannot ever, return to the old-style religion of conservative evangelicals. As a beginning for our discussion—a baseline, if you will—let me tell you the story of evangelical Erica Lyle and her family, who live in Rockwall and attend Lake Pointe Church. I'll begin the story long before Erica married her husband, Madison, because I want you to see some of the forces that have shaped her faith.

Erica was eleven when a drunk driver hit the car her father was driving. Her dad, who was not wearing a seat belt, crashed into the steering wheel, which broke his ribs, forcing them into his heart and lungs. Erica was in the seat beside him wearing a seat belt. The paramedics loaded Erica and her dad into the same ambulance. They lay side by side, head to toe. Erica could hear her father gasping for breath. She could see him fighting the paramedics as they tried to help him and couldn't because his lungs were filling with blood and no one could help. A paramedic who noticed her watching moved between Erica and her dad so that she didn't see him die.

It was Erica's grandmother who brought her to the Lord. They both were grieving. Her grandmother told Erica that if she accepted Jesus, her loss would be only temporary. She would see her father when she went to heaven, and not only that: Jesus would always be with her, always ready to comfort, always able to turn tragedy into something better. So Erica accepted Jesus into her heart and became a Christian.

She went to church, prayed every day, and did devotionals every morning. Then her mother remarried, and when Erica was a junior in high school they moved from the big city to a small West Texas town. She didn't want to move, and the transition was hard for her. She kept going to church, but the daily devotionals stopped. In a little town with nothing much to do, the kids who cruise Main Street and the back roads making their own parties on Saturday night are often the same kids who show up in church Sunday morning. Erica was among them, of course. She began to date a boy her parents didn't approve of. He was from a family with many problems, and although he was a Christian, he was having trouble finding acceptance among the church kids from more stable families. So Erica befriended him and they became a couple. It was what she now calls *missionary dating*. Her plan was that she would give him respectability enough that the church kids would embrace him.

She and her new boyfriend had some troubles, and she thought that if they had sex he would believe she trusted him. Right before graduation, Erica realized she was pregnant. She never considered abortion. A doctor suggested adoption. That wasn't an option, either. People in the church said, "She's the last girl we would have ever expected this from." She felt ashamed, foolish, and caught. Those were the consequences, she says now, just the natural consequences of sin.

"That's when life got real for me," she said. "I grew up in a hurry."

As she faced her parents and her preacher, the church folks and her peers, she felt God shielding her from the worst of the feelings. He helped her see that she was trying to manage her own life rather than following him. He let her know that this could be a turning point. Either she could continue her own way, or she could rededicate herself to him. Once again, as she had done at eleven, she chose Jesus.

Her parents opposed the marriage, but she insisted. She also insisted on starting college that fall. It wasn't long before her marriage began to fray. She says her young husband let her do most of the breadwinning. He drank more than she liked. He lost his temper. An argument got out of hand one night, and the neighbors called the police.

She moved out. Some months later, when she went back to their apartment to get her furniture, she found earrings on the nightstand and a note from a woman. The male friends who had come with her to help move furniture were nervous about how she might take the note. They didn't need to worry. To Erica those earrings and that note were just more of God's blessings.

They were an answer to her prayer that God would let her know she was making the right decision.

She filed for divorce soon after. One afternoon after church when she and some friends went to Luby's Cafeteria for lunch, she met a warmhearted, red-haired young Christian who had just come to town. His name was Madison Lyle. She took her son, Josh, on their first date and almost every date thereafter.

Madison, too, had grown up in a Christian home. He was a wild kid in high school, captain of the football team, captain of the track team, a beer-drinking carouser who made it to church every Sunday no matter how hung over he was from the night before because his dad demanded it. At eighteen, he was in church one Sunday night, and instead of drawing, as he typically did during sermons, he listened to the preacher. Having been to church two or three times a week his entire life, Madison knew the songs, knew the verses, and probably could have done most of the sermons. There wasn't much chance he would hear anything new, but he did. He must have. Something the preacher said that night touched him in a new way, and Madison accepted the Lord. Whatever it was, it changed him so much that today he says, "I would die for my faith. It means that much to me. I hope I don't have to, but I would."

Erica wasn't looking for another man. Madison wasn't looking for a ready-made family. But something was right between them. They dated for three and a half years. It took him a month to kiss her. They vowed that they wouldn't have sex until marriage. And they didn't. It was a struggle.

"We were not perfect by any means. We made mistakes," says Erica. It took planning and recommitment to their resolve and staying out of situations where having sex might begin to seem more and more likely. Their past experiences helped them there. Every night that Madison was in town, from the time Josh was two until he was five, he came over to their house after he and

Erica got off work. They had dinner together. Josh went to bed, and when Erica was ready to go to bed, Madison went home.

Their future marriage almost derailed one day when they were coming back from a visit with Madison's parents. Erica said that if she was making money and she wanted to buy a car, she would. She wouldn't consult her husband. Why should she? It was her money. Madison said that such decisions ought to be made together in a marriage, and the husband should have the final say.

Erica snapped back, "If it's my money and I want it, I'll buy it."

Madison held his tongue, but he thought, *Not if you marry me, you won't.*

The dispute got heated. Erica wasn't sure she ought to give a man too much control. Madison wasn't sure a woman as strong as Erica could be controlled. He feared she might not let him be the head of their household, and he believed God demanded that of him. Whether Erica made money or didn't make money, God would hold her husband accountable for how the money was spent.

"I had to know that she was willing to sit under my authority as head of the household," he said. Without such certainty, he wouldn't marry. Eventually, Erica came to see it his way. She agrees that he will have to stand before God to answer for his family. The ultimate responsibility is his, and so it's only right that he should have the authority he needs to obey God. Her problem, she realized, was that she didn't yet trust Madison enough. Once she began to trust, they would be ready for marriage, and not until then.

They married when Josh was still a preschooler, and now they have three young daughters, as well as Josh, who was a senior in high school and a strong contender for salutatorian when I met them. Erica sometimes calls Josh her testimony, meaning that his conception and the difficulties around it were the events that led her closer to the Lord.

Years before I met him I knew about Josh from my friend Sharon, who also lives in Rockwall. Josh is one of her son Matthew's best friends. She talked about Josh enough over the years that I remembered his name when she recommended the Lyle family as a good example of the best of Lake Pointe Church. He's the most polite, the most thoughtful, and the most Christian of Matthew's friends. But he's still considered cool, Sharon always said, one of those kids who's liked by kids and adults. If anyone in the family has been sick, Josh will remember to ask how they're doing—not a common occurrence with teenage boys.

"He's just the perfect kid," Sharon said, in her typically generous way. He's a genius, said Matthew—a National Merit scholar who doesn't hand out such accolades often.

For a model on how to raise their children, the Lyles and many other Christian conservatives look to how their parents raised them and use the Bible as their ultimate guide. If anything, the Lyles are even more conservative than their parents were. They both trick-or-treated as children, for instance, but they don't allow their children to. Their parents, who may not have believed in ghosts, goblins, and witches, never worried about the holiday, but Erica, like of a lot of evangelicals today, believes destructive supernatural powers to be actively at work in the world. It is for that reason that she has not allowed her four children to read Harry Potter books. When Josh announced that he planned to read them in college, she said mildly that he would be free to do that once he was out from under her roof. She has protested over books in the Rockwall public schools that violate her standards and would happily do so again.

At Christmas the Lyles put their holiday gifts around a manger scene that Madison and Josh built and do not put up a holiday tree. The Lyle family doesn't have cable TV, and their computer is located in the living room, where the parents can easily know what their children are doing. On Saturday nights, Josh never thinks about where he'll take a date. He and his family will be at

Lake Pointe Church's Saturday evening service. Many movies his friends see and much of the music they like are off-limits to Josh. It was not until the spring of his senior year that he attended his first rock concert. Erica researched the band before allowing him to go. He wore his "Dare to Be Drug-Free" T-shirt.

During Josh's senior year, when he back-talked to his parents, they took his car away, and he had to walk to school—a punishment his friends found horrifying, not because the school is so far away but because walking was such humiliation. When friends tried to give him a ride, Erica turned them away, saying that wasn't what she had in mind.

Even during the summer of his high school graduation, Josh was not allowed to be at a girl's house after 10 p.m. He also was not allowed to call a girl or e-mail her after that time, which his parents consider the middle of the night. Josh earned the money for his used Toyota in a town where kids often get expensive new cars as gifts. His allowance is contingent on his having completed his chores, a term that is almost unheard among Rockwall teens.

When his senior class went to Rome on spring break, Josh had to choose whether to go with them or on a mission trip to Russia. He'd been to Russia twice already, and his parents also go on Russian mission trips. He chose Russia. God is at the center of Josh's life and the life of his family. His mother tells him, "I don't want you to do what you think I want you to do; I want you to do what you think God wants you to do. I'm not always right. God may be telling you something totally different than what I'm telling you."

In an era and a social class where corporal punishment of children is rare, the Lyles believe spanking has its place for young children. Once the children get older, the parents switch to more appropriate punishments: grounding, or taking away privileges. Josh well remembers the first spanking Madison gave him. Madison, who was Erica's serious boyfriend at that point, stepped on Josh's favorite model car and broke it.

"I started crying and he spanked me. I remember it," Josh said. Madison and Erica looked surprised. They didn't remember it.

"You probably threw a fit rather than crying. I didn't put up with fit throwing very well," Madison said.

Now it was Josh who didn't remember, but Erica backed Madison up.

"That was the first spanking you got from him. It was for throwing a fit. Throwing yourself on the floor right at his feet," Erica said. Madison laughed.

Josh, a lanky boy with softly curling brown hair, didn't laugh. He looked at them solemnly with his mother's dark eyes and said nothing more. Josh speaks his mind but mildly, and I never heard him argue when his parents took the last word, which they often did in a similarly mild way.

Child-development experts might see that first spanking as the story of a man unfairly punishing a toddler who wasn't old enough to know the difference being crying and a fit. Josh might see it that way, too. But for Madison and Erica that spanking wasn't unfair. It was essential in helping teach Josh where the boundary was. He could cry, but he couldn't throw a fit. If he did, a consequence would follow. To shirk teaching that lesson would be irresponsible parenting.[1]

Madison's own dad spanked him when he was a boy. "I got my tail whipped many times. I needed it," Madison said, laughing at the memory. He has a good laugh, hearty and without malice, one that makes anyone listening smile. Madison taught junior high and high school for seven years, and the children he felt sorriest for were those whose parents didn't set boundaries. The Lyles signed forms giving the Rockwall schools permission to spank their children if need be.

When Madison was a child in small-town Texas, school spankings were administered outside the classroom door, and they didn't require a parental permission form. "I want you to tell me if you're ever paddled at school," Madison's dad always told him. When the day came that Madison was told to step into the hall for a couple of licks, he reported the event to his dad.

"He whipped me again," said the self-described former hell-raiser, laughing at the memory. "I didn't make that mistake again." Such stories are a Texas tradition, part of the rich past that ought not to be changed because it worked well then and it works still. To frown at the whippings would be to disparage the story's prime example, Madison himself, whose sturdy life testifies to the value of time-tested ways, and his dad, whom he loves and reveres. Madison's attitude is properly masculine, fun loving, and in good form within evangelical circles.

THE LYLES VALUE communication, creativity, kindness, and fairness, and employ them with their children. But like all good parents, they focus first on what they believe is most essential. For the Lyles, obeying authority, having boundaries, and accepting consequences are not only at the center of human life, they are at the center of eternal life. The central story of Christianity—that humans sinned in the Garden of Eden and their sin had to be paid for by the sacrifice of God's son—rests on the phrase "had to be paid for." That's natural law, evangelicals sometimes say. That's justice. God, in his mercy and love for humans, sent his son to die. Those who repent, accept his forgiveness, and follow him go to heaven. Those who don't, go to hell. It's a boundary. Staying on the right side is critical, which means that authority, boundaries, and consequences are critical. Authority comes from God to Madison to Erica and to the children, but so does love.

"We want our children to know that they cannot make us stop loving them," Erica said once when I had named off a variety of behaviors that might emerge as they grew older, homosexuality among them. "It goes back to 'Love the sinner, hate the sin.' In a nine-year-old it may be back-talking. In a teenager it may be rebelling, and it may be being gay later on in life, whatever. It's all still the same thing. It's sin, and we don't like the sin but we still love you."

Erica tries always to deal with herself and others in awareness of the love God has given her, which she judges to be considerable and constant. When I asked her about mother's guilt, which I've found to be pretty universal, she said, "Anything that I would feel guilty about is all covered with the blood of Jesus." And then she laughed a little, perhaps realizing how dramatic that sounded. "I mean really. I feel like I've been through a lifetime of God trying to show me that. That's kind of the culmination of everything that's happened in my life."

THE LYLES COME from a different starting place than parents outside their faith framework. God is at the center of life. He is to be obeyed. The authority of God is carried down to children through a hierarchy that must be reinforced because obedience is the key to right living. Now let's look at how differently an increasing number of parents outside conservative evangelicalism deal with issues of child rearing.

Some of my friends, whom I ought to note have teenage children who seem to be turning out as well as Josh seems to be, never use the term *back talk* with their children. If there's a disagreement between them and a child, they are likely to call it an *argument,* a term that denotes far more equality than the Lyles would probably think children and parents ought to have. Few of my friends ever spanked their children—not even so much as a slap on the hand. Instead, they explain and discuss decisions from early in their children's lives, or they remove temptations. They pay close attention to their children's developmental stages and tailor their admonitions, even their praise, to the phase the child is in.

They listen to many child-development experts and behavioral scientists and even brain researchers who look at how children learn. Child-development experts, for instance, might call the fit Josh threw when Madison stepped on his toy car not a fit but coming unglued, a meltdown, or an outburst caused by more emotion than the child can handle. The parent's primary task, they say, is not merely to set a boundary but to help the child learn to gain control of himself. Time-outs are favored over spanking in every instance because they help the child calm himself. Boundaries are important, but not as important as self-expression, good communication, and fairness.

When we compare how most American children were raised even thirty years ago with the way they are raised now, there is an astonishing difference. Linguist George Lakoff believes that parents outside conservative evangelical circles are moving away from what he calls the *strong-father model* toward a new way of looking at morality and child rearing that he calls the *nurturant model*. This model of the family, which uses empathy rather than rules or obedience to authority as the basis for morality, seems to have been empowered by feminism and women's increased voice in society, Lakoff notes. It has spread to families with two parents and even to single-father households. I found other sources who saw earlier examples of what he calls the nurturant model. They link it with upper-middle- and upper-class status rather than the influence of women.

In the nurturant model, obedience comes from love and re-spect more than fear of punishment (which, in fairness to the Lyles, is also largely true in their house, I believe). Parents' authority comes from their ability to communicate their values and reasoning. Certainly this is not only important to the Lyles, but critical to them, and they do a good job of that. The difference is that the Lyles have a prescribed set of values. Much of the rest of America is more in flux.

These new ways of child rearing help by preparing children for such a world. Children governed in the new ways are ex-pected to be kind, sensitive, self-reliant, communicative, and happy adults because they pattern themselves after their parents. God may or may not figure in the picture, which means that the parents are acting much more on their own, and their children's modeling must rely much more on the parents' behavior alone.[2]

Lakoff pairs this kind of parenting with liberal attitudes. I'm not sure he's right about that. I lived for sixteen years in such highly Republican neighborhoods that anyone voting in the Democratic primaries had to practically shake the election judges awake to cast a ballot, and I'd say such nurturant parenting is the most common form used by my neighbors. So I would not agree that only liberals have changed parenting style. When was the last time you saw a child being hit with a belt, a switch, or even a hand in public? All those pleading parents with screaming toddlers can't possibly be liberals.

Americans who aren't conservative evangelicals want almost the same things for their children as those in the religious right do. They may not put obedience to God as high as evangelicals do, and when they do, they are likely to define that obedience differently. They may not value church attendance as highly as evangelicals do, but they want their children to be good citizens and thoughtful, caring, moral people. Most hope their children will marry and stay married. They, too, want drug-free children. They, too, want their children to eschew sexual activity at a young age. They don't always expect that their children will be virgins until marriage, but many would be quite happy if their children could be persuaded to make such a decision. It often seems to be assumed among evangelicals that some families favor raunchy television and movies for their children, that some families like their children to listen to popular music filled with profanity, violence, and contempt directed toward women. Or that other parents are too weak to deal with their children. But that is rarely the case and rarely what's at stake.

What's at stake is whether children must become independent minded and able to reason through tough decisions on their own at early ages or whether they will be sheltered from such decisions until adulthood by families in which obedience to parental and godly authority is more highly valued. Parents who've changed their parenting style have come to believe that their children need new strengths as they face a rapidly changing world, and those strengths need to be developed early. For these parents, physical punishment encourages violence in later life. Bolstering the child's self-respect and autonomy is important. Being cared for and caring for others are linked. The idea that a happy, self-reliant person with adequate self-esteem is more likely to be a moral, good citizen has replaced the Christian image of humans as sinful creatures in need of outside salvation. What was once called sin is now considered sickness. So health rather than holiness is the modern parent's goal.

The loci of moral authority in the Lyles' family are the Bible, God, preachers, and other authorities—with the parents, the father foremost, as the ultimate representative of those authorities. Nurturant parents, on the other hand, employ empathy with the plight of others, writes Lakoff. So questions such as whether homosexuality is right or wrong don't rely on the Bible but on whether sexuality is chosen or inherent and whether people can live good lives if they are gay and whether it's fair to deny them the rights that heterosexuals have. Being happy is more important than being obedient. Fairness is more important than a standard of holiness. Pleasure is good, and whatever brings pleasure without hurting someone else is probably OK, writes Lakoff.

Some studies of such children show that they like their parents better and communicate with them better than previous generations as they go into teen and young-adult years. Other studies show that although they are more trying as children and may seem to lack independence, in adulthood such children are better prepared for the complex kinds of thought and communication that are needed in the work world. Contrasting studies show that modern children are in trouble because parents aren't setting good boundaries or are relying on praise rather than high standards as a way to gain self-esteem. The verdict is not yet in. As Lakoff points out, either type of parenting can veer into problems and be bad, or either can be good.

So why did so many parents believe such a radical shift was necessary? I've already noted that experts and research played a part, but it was more than that. Science and democracy demand questioning, observing, and reasoning as ways of finding truth. Ambiguity is now seen as part of the process of learning enough about the world to thrive and is not seen as something that needs to be abolished. Simple answers are suspect as wrong answers. Change is embraced. Tradition is devalued because in a rapidly changing world it doesn't yield the benefits it once did. The ability to challenge authority is important to a society based on democracy and science. The ability to take in great amounts of conflicting information is important to creativity.

And, of course, many people don't believe in God as strongly as was once common. If they do believe in God, they may not be certain that they know much about him. In such cases, telling your children to do what God wants and not what you want, as the Lyles do, wouldn't make a bit of sense.

Travel, communication, and immigration have sped up these changes by giving legitimacy to new ideas that we once would have rejected out of hand. As a result, all sorts of cultural shibboleths are toppling. The moral relativism that conservative Christians decry might be seen as a direct result of empathic morality—not only in child rearing but in all of society. As I've already noted, it seems as if a new way of judging what's moral and what's not is coming into being. The old version was based on tradition and religious rules. The new one is based on empathy, which always employs situational ethics along with moral guidelines rather than strict rules. What does that mean for evangelical growth? It means that people don't feel the same need for the kind of God evangelical faith supplies. They don't feel the need for the same kind of rules. In fact, they see those rules as impediments to a healthy life, which is the standard that has replaced the holy, obedient, or righteous life that evangelicals pursue.

So the kind of God evangelicals worship is devalued by children raised in the nurturant model because they don't think of themselves as sinful or even as particularly disempowered. The leap of faith and the unquestioning obedience to biblical rules that evangelical faith rests on are also devalued—replaced by questioning, self-scrutiny, logic, and reasoning. Nurturant parents have rewarded these qualities from their children's earliest memories by giving explanations, encouraging dissent, and giving way when their children are able to convince them that they are wrong. Even the new types of punishment that nurturant parents use aim not at obedience, or even setting a boundary, but at allowing the child to gain self-control and make better decisions for himself.

So when an evangelical tells these children that they are sinful and in need of saving, ignorant and in need of truth, they don't respond as generations in the past might have. They think of themselves as healthy or unhealthy. Achieving health requires a change in behavior, not a total reorientation of one's inner being. They are less likely to privilege divine revelation unless that revelation comes to them. And even if it has, they've been taught from their earliest ages that one person's revelation ought to be challenged, ought be examined in light of all verifiable facts and reasonable arguments. This kind of thinking, which was once the purview of adults only, is now being taught to children. It makes them flexible, thinking, reasoning, searching people. Obnoxious sometimes. Not always wise. But fundamentally different in how they think of themselves and others than many Americans of previous generations were. Belief in supernatural providence isn't an impossibility. Some of them may be quite devout, but for them to become unquestioning followers of in-flexible evangelical rules, more concerned about righteousness than equality or fairness, would be impossible.

I know how impossible it would be because I was raised with a foot in each camp. I learned that humans are sinful and in need of salvation, but at the same time my mother was more often a reasoner than a spanker. She rarely demanded that I do anything because she was the adult and I was the child. She valued my ideas and protected my dignity. My dad believed in knowledge, in the pursuit of culture and learning, and in the value of asking the right question even if other people thought it was irrelevant.

I was saved in the Baptist church because I had a grounding in the old ways. I left the Baptist church because my mental habits were formed by the ways of my parents. One of the most potent lessons I learned came from talking with my mother about the rules she put down for me. Again and again, she would tell me how something was to be done and why. I would listen and think and then come back to her and say, "But that isn't all there is to it. There's also this and this and this." And my mother would listen, and she would often say, "You're right. It is more complicated."

"You're right. It is more complicated" was permission to use my mind. To think, to challenge, to win the day. Parents are the first gods in our lives. When they say from our earliest memo-ries, "You're right. It is more complicated," in response to our scrutiny of the rules, it's impossible to respect or love a God who would do less. And so although the gifts and strengths of evan-gelical faith—Van Grubbs's sure knowledge of who he is, what he is to do, and how he is to act; Michelle and Mike Tauzin's transformation from friendless and alone to blessed and loved; Susan Bruk's sense of being protected by a God so strong that even death cannot defeat him—are wondrous, they weren't enough for me. And already it is becoming clear that they aren't enough for the young people of today.

Ample research documents that new generations' opinions of Christianity are a "punch in the gut" to evangelical faith, write evangelicals Kinnaman and Lyons in *UnChristian*.[3] The vast majority of them don't need to hear the Good News. They have been exposed to Christianity in an astonishing number of ways, and that's exactly why they're rejecting it. They react negatively to "'our swagger,' how we go about things, and the sense of self-importance we project," the evangelicals write. One young outsider is quoted as saying, "Most people I meet assume that Christian means very conservative, entrenched in their thinking, antigay, antichoice, angry, violent, illogical, empire builders; they want to convert everyone, and they generally cannot live peacefully with anyone who doesn't believe what they believe."[4]

Robert Wuthnow's conclusions about young America are slightly different, and alarming for evangelicals in another way. The proportion of younger adults who are evangelicals has declined for three decades, he writes. Statistics that show America's young falling in line with core beliefs of evangelicals should offer little comfort, Wuthnow writes, because younger Americans are what he calls "tinkerers." They may keep a core of beliefs but are always open to new ideas and feel free to amend their beliefs continuously as conversations with friends, reflections, experiences, or even songs persuade them to view issues differently. The notion that they ought to be "updating" their beliefs is an important part of their spiritual quest. Evangelicals' steady loss of young people causes Wuthnow, one of the most respected religion scholars in America, to deride the very idea that evangelicals are the vibrant, growing, unstoppable force they have been seen as. He writes, "They are certainly not the numeric powerhouse they sometimes imagine themselves to be."[5]

End of Chpt. 13

Fourteen

WHAT HAPPENS NEXT?

Evangelical faith has survived many downturns in the past. Great Awakenings have swept the country, and the number of believers has rebounded. That could happen again, but it would take a miracle from God—such an enormous and unlikely miracle that even many evangelicals don't think it's going to happen. Thus a lot of talk in the Christian community at large is circling around the idea that a new Reformation might be due. The original one began about six hundred years ago as the printing press helped democratize Christianity by making the Bible more widely available. Some evangelicals think the Internet is having a similar effect in allowing people to think differently about Christianity.

During the first Reformation, human beings were getting access to Scripture. This time they're getting unbrokered access to each other. For the first time, evangelicals have a safe, easily available, and anonymous place to ask the questions and express the doubts that they wouldn't dare admit face-to-face with other evangelicals. The Internet's lack of authority figures is heightening the effect, writes Spencer Burke, a former evangelical megachurch pastor who set up a Web site, www.theooze.com, that attracts a quarter of a million viewers a month. Part of the Internet's democratization is that it does away with status, position, age, race, and appearance, according to Burke. People are judged solely on the strength of their ideas.

For evangelicals that means that the traditional markers for knowing whether it's all right to accept a new idea are gone. They can gather at any time to exchange ideas, and decide for themselves or together whether something is true or false, of God or not of God. All three stories of evangelical defectors told earlier in this book showed examples of how exposure to other thinking and experiences is pushing people out of the fold. The effect might be something like what happened to Jay, the closeted gay evangelical husband, who went to a Christian group hoping to get rid of homosexual urges and instead found other Christians who understood him better than any he'd met before. As a result he turned away from his old life and toward a new one.

The Internet itself was heavily involved in the other two stories. Cathy, the Pentecostal, was shaken by her son's admission that he didn't believe, urged on by a newspaper article, but when she went looking for answers, she felt that God provided a path—through the Internet. Helen, the Chicago woman who took a vacation from talking to God, began to talk with atheists on the Internet instead. They assured her that the scare stories her evangelical friends told her weren't true.

Not all evangelicals want to leave the faith. Some want to reform it, and the Internet gives them a big audience. Spencer Burke is among a growing number of evangelicals who are beginning to move away from the idea that only they are saved. His newest book, promoted on his Web site, is called *A Heretic's Guide to Eternity*. I met him at a conference put on by Jim Henderson, another evangelical with similar interests, who is gathering a group based on Internet contact through his Web site, www.off-themap.com. At the conference, Spencer always seemed to be at the center of a group of young, hip-looking men. He looks like a sort of Christian Robin Williams. He has the same stocky build and brown hair, and he wears T-shirts with loose-fitting casual pants that include many pockets. He puts off the same sparky intelligence and energy that Williams does, without the jokes. The entire time we talked, his right leg jiggled.

A former hippie who was saved as a young adult, Spencer lived in a Christian commune for a while, entered the ministry, and worked his way up to being the teaching pastor at a mega-church. The teaching pastor at a megachurch is second in command and a major voice for the church. Spencer quit that job. His heresy in *A Heretic's Guide to Eternity* is that he believes in hell but doesn't think anyone has to do anything to keep from going there. He thinks Jesus's sacrifice paid for everybody: Buddhists, Hindus, atheists—everybody.

"You only go to hell if you opt out," he said.

"How do you opt out?"

"I don't know. Nobody knows," he said. "You're not supposed to know."

I told him that I've noticed Americans moving to a different ethic based on the Golden Rule, a.k.a. empathy. He sees that, too.

"The amazing part to me is that we opted out of that evangelical thinking," I said. By *we,* I meant the culture as a whole. "We all used to be like the evangelicals. Not so long ago. Now we aren't. We think they're the strange ones. I'm part of it myself. I opted out."

"And if we hadn't, we'd all be just like they are," he said. "Angry, judgmental, narrow, mean. Look at where things are now." Americans torturing other people. Going to war. Wrecking the environment. We would all be going along with those things if we hadn't changed. The trajectory of fundamentalism was set a long time ago. The only option was to opt out or go along, he said.

Angry, judgmental, narrow, mean.

"But not all the people are," I said.

"No, not the people," he said. "The institutions." The institutions carry everyone along and frame what's happening.

"If we'd kept thinking the same old way, we would all be like that," Spencer said. And getting worse.

New ideas are also being put about by a group called the emerging church. One of their most well known leaders is Brian McLaren, who was also at the conference. One of his books, *A New Kind of Christian,* startled evangelicals with the idea that not everyone had to think as traditional evangelicals do in order to follow Christ. It became a bestseller. Jim Henderson, the evangelical I mentioned earlier who is trying to convince Christians that being kind is a way of witnessing for Christ, is getting good sales with a book called *Jim and Casper Go to Church,* in which he takes an atheist to churches around the country and listens to his criticisms. Jim's new evangelical ideas include a term I'd never heard: *beliefism.* It's a slur on what he calls the "worship of right beliefs." Instead, Jim talks about a Christianity of "doing" that rests on actions and attitudes, which gives him a lot in common with some of Barna's revolutionaries.

Not long ago on a plane from Dallas to Los Angeles, I sat next to one of them, an evangelical businessman who is heavily involved in foreign mission work centering around farming in Africa. He has traveled to many of the world's hot spots helping set up schools and give away books. He and his wife once brought girls from topless bars into their home and helped them start different lives. We talked all three hours of the flight. Although this revolutionary isn't leaving the church, he counts himself among the people Barna describes as wanting to live their faith all the time in every way possible and said Barna's term *revolutionary* fit him well.

He and Jim Henderson both talk about what Jim calls "heart-born, organic faith." I wasn't clear how far the revolutionary would go with the idea. He was somewhat vague, also saying that he had to follow the Bible and quoting Jesus's words that he is the way, the truth, and the light and no man comes to the Father except by him. Hoping to clarify, I gave him the gist of what Jim had once written me in an e-mail.

"I hope that God is closer to all of us than we imagine," he wrote. "I think we all make it too hard. I mean just stop and ask yourself if I made people who wanted to know me jump through the psychological hoops religionists have put in the way of people trying to locate God—what kind of weird person would that make me? It's got to be simpler than that because Jesus is God and is accessible to those who open their minds and hearts to him (at least that's my simple paradigm which, of course, I could be completely wrong about and the religionists could be right in which case I will spend my time in eternity in hell.)"

I left out the eternity-in-hell part. The revolutionary nodded and said, "I'd agree with that." Then, like so many other evangelicals, he said he doesn't particularly like being called an evangelical. "I'd rather be called a connector or a broker."

"Between people and God?" I asked. "Between people and other people?"

He nodded.

If evangelicals give up the idea that only they are saved and that hell doesn't await everyone who disagrees with them, they will be a very different faith group. It will be a struggle to keep religious passion high without the threat of hell to spark it, a struggle to keep devotion steady without the allure of being the only ones whom God favors. But some of these new-style followers of Jesus believe they have something to offer that transcends such doctrine, something that has changed them, something that is with them still, something that can change the earth.

Him.

Many of them believe that mainline Christians' problems came from pulling too far away from teaching the Bible and from the idea of a living Christ who has relationships with people. They think that if they keep those elements, they can let go of some of the other doctrinal elements that have become stumbling blocks in conversion. One group calling itself Red-Letter Christians has formed around the idea of following the words of Jesus (printed in red in some Bibles) in preference to the words of Paul, whose influence on the Christian church is so strong that some say he was actually the founder of Christianity. Some scholars believe that the Red-Letter Christians, along with people in house churches and in the emergent church, constitute up to 35 percent of evangelicals. Their Jesus is angry about the many respects in which the American way and the conservative evangelical way have come together.

"The red letters challenge Americans' justifications for accumulating wealth, support of capital punishment, ready endorsement of war, rampant consumerism, rebellion against sexual prohibitions that have sustained purity and modesty for generations, and arrogant use of economic power to fulfill national self-interests to the detriment of other nations," says the Reverend Tony Campolo, who wrote *Letters to a Young Evangelical.*

"We are evangelicals who want to change the world," he continues, "but not through political coercion. Our methodology is loving persuasion. We don't want power; we just want to speak truth to power. Frankly, we evangelicals are troubled by the political power that fundamentalists are wielding these days."[1]

Change isn't happening only on the edges of the conservative evangelical world. During the months I wrote and researched, many established conservative evangelicals themselves were changing. I've noted already that helping the poor was far more important to them than it had been a decade earlier, when I'd last looked at their practices. Whether that change has come from God or from changing demographics or both, it could redeem the good name of evangelical faith in the eyes of many outsiders. Such good works, especially if they are done without heavy-handed proselytizing, are compelling examples of what outsiders think Christians ought to be.

Steve Stroope believes concern for others is arising as evangelicals and their churches gain Christian maturity. He doesn't mince words about the harder times that may be ahead for evangelical faith if churches don't change.

"Sometimes there's a death, before there's new life," he said, but he believes a revival is sweeping through evangelical ranks, moving people away from religion as merely an institutional practice toward relationships marked by compassion. In a recent sermon outlining where Lake Pointe ought to be heading in the next three years, he told his congregation, "Be Jesus." To me he quoted Saddleback's Rick Warren, author of the multi-million-selling *The Purpose Driven Life,* as having said that evangelicals, biblically charged to be the body of Christ, have been mostly the mouth. Now they need to concentrate on being the hands and feet.

Warren has not only taken on the fight against AIDS, but has also begun to broaden his congregation's perspectives in other ways. He invited Democrat Barack Obama to his church, which caused considerable anger within the religious right because Obama supports abortion rights and gay rights. But Warren didn't back down. At the end of Obama's speech, Warren's congregation gave the presidential candidate a standing ovation.

A broad array of evangelicals, including Warren, are working to stop global warming. The National Association of Evangelicals went against the long-standing evangelical idea that personal conversion was the only godly way to bring about social change by calling for both conversion and "institutional renewal and reform." *Christianity Today,* a leading evangelical magazine, reminded its readers that "George W. Bush is not Lord."[2] The *New York Times* ran a story about a suburban St. Paul evangelical church that was split when its preacher, Gregory A. Boyd, declined to let his church be used for political purposes. At the end of the story, the preacher was quoted as saying, "All good, decent people want good and order and justice. Just don't slap the label 'Christian' on it." I haven't heard that kind of talk from evangelicals in how many years? I can't remember when. Maybe never.

Even evangelicals at the heart of the group's political power are admitting that their core truths might not be the only ones a Christian could hold. "Very honest people read the same Bible and come out with different emphases," Barrett Duke, vice president for public policy of the Southern Baptist Convention's Ethics and Religious Liberty Commission was quoted as telling the Associated Baptist Press. "People prioritize issues in different ways. If your principal priority is concern for the poor, someone might actually support abortion rights because that person considers poverty a higher priority than concern for life. And if you have conflicting priorities just in light of the fact that you have to prioritize, you might have a deep concern for women in poverty who find themselves with an unexpected pregnancy, but don't think they should abort because of a higher concern for life."[3]

So evangelicals are changing. Not because they are as powerful as we have been led to believe, but perhaps because they are not. For the past thirty years, 7 percent of the population has swayed elections and positioned itself as the ultimate arbiter of right and wrong. By puffing its numbers and its authority, it has gotten legislation passed that opposes the popular will and has divided the country into acrimonious camps. It has monopolized the media so effectively that other religious voices have been all but silenced. It has been feared and loathed, revered and loved. It has been impossible to ignore. But underneath its image of power and pomp, the evangelical nation is falling apart. Every day the percentage of evangelicals in America decreases, a loss that began more than one hundred years ago. If current trends continue, the evangelicals who remain will be poorer, browner, and more urban, which means in the short term that the concerns of the evangelical voter will change. Delivering what is now thought of as the purely Republican conservative evangelical vote will not be as easy in lower-income groups, and the focus of concern will change. In the long term, as those groups rise socially and economically, they, too, will cast off old ways of faith.

Knowing that religious-right evangelicals make up only one out of fourteen Americans doesn't eliminate the so-called religion gap in politics. People of all denominations who say they attend church weekly are more likely to vote Republican than Democratic. Many American voters are religious people with moral concerns, but the range of their moral concerns is wider, more open to new solutions, and more open to new information than that of a stereotypical religious-right evangelical voter would be. It's often been noted that Americans would never elect an atheist as president. That's probably true, but recent polls indicate it isn't specific beliefs that Americans care about. It's rather that they think candidates ought to have some belief in God as a moral underpinning for their actions.

Certain readers will rejoice at the idea that old-style evangelical faith is dying away; others will grieve. I have some of both emotions. I disagree with many evangelical ideas and fear their effects. At the same time, losing the evangelical way takes away one good way for facing life with resourcefulness and hope. Human beings need every method they can find for that.

I can hear my evangelical friends and family protesting that the decline of evangelical faith means far more than the disappearance of an earthly resource; it means that more humans will go to hell. I can't dispute that. It may be true. It may not. I know too much about human assumptions, ignorance, and bias to end all discussion as one women did by saying, "The Bible seems clear about that." I don't trust myself or anyone else to say what the Word of God actually means. It isn't a simple issue of whether I do or don't believe in the Bible. The issue is that my belief isn't of much consequence. It there a truth? Certainly. Can I know it? Not with certainty. Believing that I am stronger, wiser, or more discerning than any human can be doesn't make it so.

So if I can't know the truth about such lofty matters, what can I do to add to the store of knowledge? I can tell one of my own stories—my testimony, if you will—and perhaps you will understand why I believe that something of value to humankind will be lost if evangelical faith dies out. William James says conversion occurs when the focus of a person's concerns shifts so completely that she is not the same and a new life begins. That happened to me when I was nine years old. It happened again more than a decade after I had left the Baptist faith never to return. I was thirty-six, divorced, and in despair. A perfect candidate for God's grace.

I was so beaten up by a decade of modern dating that I feared I would never be able to love anyone with anything like the unselfishness that love needs. Each boyfriend seemed to leave me tougher, more self-centered, and less able to risk. The man I was dating obviously loved me. I didn't think I loved him despite my being so lonely that as I walked through the streets of my neighborhood at night I sometimes looked at people in the brightly lighted houses and thought that I would never have such a place in life.

One evening when I was out of town, my wretchedness boiled over with such ferocity that I broke down in the old religious way I'd heard talked about so many times in my youth, in the way William James says it takes for the ego to step aside and the unconscious to begin unifying a shattered life. I didn't know about William James then, but I did know about the Baptist way, so I prayed. I didn't pray that God would cause me to fall in love with this new boyfriend. I just prayed that he would open my shut-down heart so that I could love someone.

I planned to tell my current boyfriend that all bets were off as soon as I got home. Well, not immediately. If he wanted to take me to dinner, I'd put my announcement off a little longer. I was a real prize, as you can see. The whole focus of my life was figuring out how to get the world—usually that meant men—to do the things that would make me feel special. Sometimes that meant adoration, sometimes it meant presents, sometimes it meant doing other things I wanted. I don't want to sell myself short; I gave a lot back. Often too much. The point is that I was never satisfied because it isn't possible for a person so focused on herself to be satisfied. But that's a spiritual lesson, and I was a long way from learning it.

I'd been visiting my parents when my moment of crisis and prayer came. On the plane trip back home a ponytailed earring wearer caught my eye as he swaggered down the aisle. He smiled. I looked away. Definitely potential there. I felt that old tingle. But this time, I examined it instead of just feeling it. Was that attraction? No, that was fear. Mr. Ponytail was trouble, and I was intrigued by the opportunity of taking trouble on.

When I got off the plane, my ride home was waiting. He had a single red rose in his hand. As I walked closer, I saw that his thumb was bleeding.

"What happened to you?" I asked.

"I stabbed myself picking off the thorns," he said.

I took the rose and kissed him. What else could I do? As I leaned over, I caught sight of Mr. Ponytail watching. He shrugged, gave me a little salute, and walked away.

The other eleven roses were in the front seat of the car. I wish I could tell you that I was transformed and grateful when I saw them, but I wasn't. All I thought was that I didn't really care for red roses. Yellow was more my color. We had dinner. I said I was tired and wanted to go home. He asked if we could stop by the bookstore next door. As we were standing in front of a bookshelf, he reached out and gently touched my shoulder. It was as though a spark went through me. I don't mean static electricity. It was some kind of twinkling transformation such as a fairy godmother might accomplish with her wand. Rags into a ball gown, a pumpkin into a coach, white mice into footmen. My date went from nice enough into "Well, well, what have we here?" His touch startled me as though I had been suddenly awakened. I snapped around to look at him, and he wasn't the same. He was not just another boyfriend soon to pass on, as he had been a second ago. He had turned into a person. It was perhaps the first time in my life that any man had seemed like a real person to me. I mean a person in the same way women are people. Men were something else, fearsome objects that might or might not do what I wanted them to. We were married four months from that night in the bookstore, and from then to now I've been happier than ever before in my life.

Here are the facts as I experienced them. I prayed; I changed; I gained all that I'd hoped for. So perhaps it won't seem too unreasonable of me to have given God the credit. I couldn't help perceiving a link, but that moment of transformation, important as it was, was not the most miraculous thing that happened.

Because I thought that God had put his stamp of approval on my new husband, I was no longer a consumer of love looking for the best deal I could make. I had been liberated from the American trap of having so many choices that nothing seems quite good enough. It is only a little bit of an exaggeration to say that I felt divinely committed, and that was the real miracle. Whenever I was disappointed or angry with my husband, instead of lashing out or sinking into despair as I once would have done, I reflected on how this love had been so miraculously given to me. Because it felt destined, I tried harder to be fair and kind and not selfish. An entire system of good behavior, modeled on Jesus's life as presented in the most conservative evangelical fashion, went into effect. Perhaps the best part of it was the gratitude. I'd been raised to believe that gratitude was the proper response for every good thing in life. My "miracle" activated that old lesson, which put me in just the right spot for happiness.

I don't mind if you credit a William Jamesian moment of surrender instead of God's grace and believe that my conscious self stepped aside and my wiser, unconscious self emerged to set things right. Mysterious, wondrous things happen to all sorts of people who have all sorts of belief systems or no belief systems at all, and so if you wish to believe that the universe heard my cry and answered, or that a passing genie heard my wish and followed me home to work some magic, I'm fine with all that. You could even believe that what happened in the bookstore was a random event or the result of a particularly good dinner working its way through my digestive system, or that it didn't happen at all, that I made it up. I don't care, because the important point is that when something good happened, I hooked it to a larger story, the story of God's intervention, and because I did that, my transformative moment had a trajectory.

That moment, which I could have called luck or serendipity or lust or anything else, I called God, and calling it God connected me to an ancient, wisdom-filled path lined with symbols and sayings, promises and pitfalls that were intertwined with my family, my heritage, my deepest self. I had grown up in a faith tradition which teaches that God is intimately connected with our lives, a tradition that assured me he would hear and respond to my prayers and that if I followed his leading, I would be living in the best way possible. I would be happy beyond any happiness that my own wisdom could secure for me. And that was what happened.

I did not enter that path in the same way I had when I was nine years old. In fact, by most evangelical reckonings I didn't get back on the path at all. I still have all the doubts and disagreements that led me away from church, stronger than ever. I don't go to church and perhaps never will. I don't read the Bible. I pray only if I want to. I'm not an evangelical and don't want to be one. But my life was made immeasurably better by some of the truths evangelicals taught me. The power of those truths stayed with me even though I never signed on again. The same is true for many people. And so I am not entirely sanguine about the notion that the evangelical way of faith is dying, but I am hopeful about some good things it could lead to.

The kind of divisive politics that have riven the country for thirty years may ease, and Americans may once again be able to speak civilly about moral issues. The level of rancor and ill will among people who all want the best for the country may go down. People's sex lives and the personhood of stem cells might stop dominating moral discussions so completely, allowing Americans to deal with other moral concerns: health care, poverty, injustice.

People who fear talking openly about their atheism or even merely about their doubts would be freer to discuss ideas. America's strong streak of self-righteousness—often displayed in international affairs, to the dismay of other countries—might lose its religious endorsement. Manifest destiny, the idea that the United States is a specially favored nation with the God-given right to expand its territory no matter how many native people it kills, would no longer have the sanctuary it has had. Politicians would be careful to keep hidden any notion that they had been chosen by God to take power.

The cultural slowdown that evangelical opposition offers to many progressive ideas, such as embryonic stem-cell research, euthanasia, gay rights, drug legalization, and abortion rights, would be weakened, and change might speed up. The tug-of-war between the past and the future, between the values and ways of being that most Americans held fifty years ago and those they are beginning to hold, would become more lopsided. The moral cover that evangelicals offer for governmental programs that hurt the poor would be less effective, but the powerful life-changing conversions they offer people in trouble might also become less common.

To recognize that the most conservative forms of evangelical faith are dwindling and have been for a hundred years dissolves a delusion about who we are as Americans. Once we realize that we are a far more varied group of people than the religious right would like us to believe, perhaps we can enter into real conversation about what morality is and what it isn't today, not what it was two thousand years ago for a patriarchal tribal society, but what it is or ought to be today for a world power in a nuclear, environmentally threatened age, an age in which sexual habits were irrevocably changed by birth-control methods and half the population was freed from compulsory childbearing.

This recognition can allow other religious and nonreligious voices to be heard. It can allow women's voices to be heard in spiritual settings where conservative evangelicals can never allow them. Acknowledging that such people also have moral, ethical, and spiritual wisdom that needs to be listened to would be almost impossible in a country where a quarter of the people are conservative evangelicals with ownership of moral and religious truth. But we are not in that kind of country. Knowing that we don't live in such a country might even help those of us who feel shut out of faith to reconnect with God in ways that serve our time and place better than the old ways.

It's happened before. It could happen again.

End of chpt. 14

NOTES ⟩ *gres to fg. 214*

CHAPTER 2: ONE OUT OF FOUR AMERICANS?

1. Surveys of church attendance by religious organizations can also have problems. One possible problem comes in defining what a regular attendee is. For instance, a study published in 2007 by the Southern Baptists shows that churches can make subtle shifts that cause numbers to look better than perhaps they ought to. Instead of the common question *Have you been to church in the last seven days?* this study asked teens if they had been to church in the last thirty days. Fifty-four percent said they had, and those were considered churchgoing teens. That can be justified by saying that families have more to do on Sundays now and so attendance has become more sporadic and asking if they'd been to church that week would be an inaccurate number. But along with less church time comes less knowledge about core beliefs and probably less commitment. I haven't used that development in my primary argument about the fall of evangelical faith only because it's a development that affects all faiths. But it's an important change in Christian practice and may affect religious-right evangelicals more than others because their doctrines require special emphases that members won't get anywhere else in the culture.

The lack of church time showed up in the Southern Baptist survey when the teens were queried about their beliefs. Only 28 percent trusted only in Jesus as a way to get to heaven, which is evangelical bedrock. Sixty percent thought that Jesus was the way but that they would also go to heaven because they were kind to others or merely religious. The study also showed that since 2005 the number of teens who believed in heaven at all dropped 6 percent, from 75 percent to 69 percent.

2. The African-American Church of God in Christ, with 5.5 million members, is the next-largest evangelical/Pentecostal denomination, but our focus is on evangelicals who constitute the backbone of the religious-right political and social movement. For that reason I'm considering only white evangelicals and using the Assemblies of God, which reports 2.8 million members. Although African-American evangelicals may share opposition to gay rights and to abortion rights with their white counterparts, they differ from them on many other social and political issues and wouldn't be automatically considered part of the religious right. These numbers come from the *Yearbook of American and Canadian Churches* (Nashville: Abingdon Press, 2007).

3. Some of those churches don't have adult Sunday school or small groups. But since those churches that did give figures showed half their members in these groups, I used the total membership of NAE churches, 7.6 million, with half of those, 3.8 million, counted as core members—a generous assessment.

Scott Thumma and Dave Travis's *Beyond Megachurch Myths: What We Can Learn from America's Largest Churches* (San Francisco: Jossey-Bass, 2007) shows a higher percentage of committed members in megachurches. Thumma and Travis believe that about 60 percent of megachurch participants are strongly committed to their churches and the doctrines they teach. But the Sunday school rule of 50 percent for the NAE total still seems appropriate for two reasons. Megachurches are renowned for the commitment they get from members. So their percentage of committed members is likely to be higher than most churches'. In addition, Thumma and Travis's research shows that 5 percent of the megachurch congregation are the church's core leaders and another 15 percent are its firmly committed, who give a lot of time and money to the church. So it could be argued that the religious-right evangelicals we're looking for

make up between 20 percent and 60 percent of megachurch attendance. Certainly no more. We could split the difference and say
they're 40 percent, but once again, I'll use the greater number of 50
percent to give the religious right every member it might possibly
have.

4. For an interesting look at this issue of civic religion and how it di-
verges from Jesus's teachings, see Gregory A. Boyd's *The Myth of a
Christian Nation: How the Quest for Political Power Is Destroying
the Church* (Grand Rapids, MI: Zondervan, 2007). Stephen Prothero's
American Jesus: How the Son of God Became a National Icon (New
York: Farrar, Straus and Giroux, 2003) also provides some interesting sidelights on the issue.

CHAPTER 4: IN THE YEAR OF "EVERYONE CAN!" EVERYONE DIDN'T

1. Princeton's Robert Wuthnow challenges the popular idea that liberal
doctrine and lax standards hurt the mainliners. In his book *After the
Baby Boomers* he contends that most of the loss in mainline
churches' membership has come not because of doctrine but because
of declining birthrates that haven't yet hit evangelicals. If he's right,
evangelicals are bound for the same fate. As their income and educa-
tion level rise, they, too, will see members delaying marriage longer
and having fewer children when they do marry.

2. "Left Behind: The Skewed Representation of Religion in Major New
Media," Media Matters for America, www.mediamatters.org/.

3. Diane Winston, "Press Coverage of Religion Tilts to the Right,"
Huffington Post, June 7, 2007, www.huffingtonpost.com/.

4. In addition, the number of Americans who refused to answer the religion question also grew from 1990 to 2001. The number was 5
million, or 2 percent, in 1990, and 11 million, or 5 percent, in 2001.
Both sets of statistics are from the American Religious Identification
Survey. If we put those who refuse to answer with those who claim
no faith, we would have 40 million Americans.

I don't question these statistics as I've questioned church-membership
statistics and people who identify themselves as evangelicals because
it seems less likely that those who say they have no religion would
exaggerate their lack of belief. Some people might argue that point,
especially considering the reputation that Christians seem to have—
which is a topic I'll look at in later chapters. But having no faith
doesn't seem to confer a particular societal advantage or guilt feeling

that might cause a person to distort their actual beliefs when talking to a pollster. Those who refuse to answer are also unlikely to be closet evangelicals because they are so firmly taught that refusing to claim Christian belief is a denial of Jesus.

Nevertheless, I use these statistics only as a way of giving perspective on what's actually happening in the country. If they were part of my main argument, I would look into them more closely.

5. Norm Miller, "1,900 Professions of Faith Flow from One Woman's Witness," *Baptist Press*, May 2006.
6. Libby Lovelace, "Encouragement for Evangelism: LifeWay Research Studies 19 Standout Churches," January 30, 2007, LifeWay Research, www.lifeway.com.
7. Thumma and Travis, *Beyond Megachurch Myths*, 125.

The Southern Baptist Convention's North American Mission Board report based on the 2001 U.S. Congregational Life Survey found almost the same number. Transfers, switchers, or returners accounted for all but 8 percent of those who had been in churches fewer than five years.

8. Jones, *Analysis of Southern Baptist Churches*.
9. Libby Lovelace, "The New View of Young Adults," LifeWay Research, December 12, 2006, www.lifeway.com.

CHAPTER 6: SINNERS ONE AND ALL

1. Ronald J. Sider, *The Scandal of the Evangelical Conscience: Why Are Christians Living Just Like the Rest of the World?* (Grand Rapids, MI: Baker Books, 2005), 17.
2. Sider, 22.
3. Hanna Rosen, "Even Evangelical Teens Do It," *Slate*, May 30, 2007.
4. David Kinnaman and Gabe Lyons, *UnChristian: What a New Generation Really Thinks about Christianity* (Grand Rapids, MI: Baker Books, 2007), 52.
5. "Trends in Political Values and Core Attitudes, 1987–2007: Political Landscape More Favorable to Democrats," Pew Research Center for the People and the Press, March 22, 2007, http://people-press.org/reports/pdf/312.pdf.
6. Ted Olsen, "Go Figure," *Christianity Today*, October 20, 2006, and April 18, 2007.

CHAPTER 7: GIANTS CRASHING

1. John L. Ronsvalle and Sylvia Ronsvalle, *The State of Church Giving Through 2004* (Champaign, IL: empty tomb, 2006).

2. That's one picture of the buster generation. Even more dismal characterizations of them come from Robert Wuthnow's *After the Baby Boomers.* His statistics show a generation that's slow to settle down, slow to have children, and prone to individualizing their spirituality. He sees what he calls their "tinkering" approach to life resulting in 6 million fewer church members. If church leaders don't figure out how to draw these generations in, the future of religion in America is threatened, he writes. David Kinnaman and Gabe Lyons's *unChristian: What a New Generation Really Thinks About Christianity . . . and Why It Matters* (Grand Rapids, MI: Baker Books, 2007) portrays a similar crisis brewing. Late teens to early thirtysomethings believe that Christians are judgmental, homophobic, hypocritical, too political, and isolated, Kinnaman and Lyons write.

CHAPTER 8: SCATTERING OF THE FAITHFUL

1. Rebecca Barnes and Lindy Lowry, "Special Report: American Church in Crisis," *Outreach,* May/June 2006.

2. E-mail communication, July 7, 2007.

CHAPTER 9: DISILLUSIONED BELIEVERS

1. Todd Johnson, "USA Evangelicals in Global Context: Trends and Statistics," table for *Encyclopedia Britannica* by the Center for the Study of Global Christianity at Gordon-Conwell Theological Seminary. These statistics are based on various polls, surveys, and census reports. Like other such statistics, they rely mainly on self-reports that may or may not include questions that help identify evangelicals by belief. As an example of how much using questions changes the number of self-identified evangelicals, Gallup found 42 percent of Americans calling themselves born again or evangelical in 2003. In 2005, the pollster asked three questions to identify born-agains and evangelicals: 1. Born again experience? 2. Witness for Christ? 3. Bible as literal Word of God? The percentage dropped to 19 percent.

2. Methodology for rough estimate from Todd Johnson (director, Center for the Study of Global Christianity at Gordon-Conwell

Theological Seminary), e-mail correspondence with author, July 20, 2007.

3. Statistics from the Center for the Study of Global Christianity show that the percentage of Christians in the United States increases by about fifty-four hundred every day, which is slightly less than population growth. That means that each day the United States becomes less Christian. Among the factors increasing the number of Christians are babies born to Christians (ninety-five hundred), non-Christians converting to Christianity (fifty-five hundred), and Christians immigrating to the United States from other countries (twenty-two hundred). For the purposes of this book, which is to look at the type of evangelicals driving social and political change (a type I've sometimes referred to as religious-right-type evangelicals, who are overwhelmingly white), these statistics are another blow. As I pointed out earlier, nonwhite evangelicals often don't share many values that drive the current religious-right agenda. Christians immigrating to the United States and many non-Christians converting to Christianity, who number seventy-seven hundred by this estimate, will exert their own influence on the evangelical voice and likely change it considerably.

4. Erik Tryggestad, "Are We Losing Our Young People?" *Christian Chronicle*, June 19, 2007.

5. Rhoda Tse, "Studies Show Once Students Graduate from High School They Struggle with Their Faith," *Christian Post*, January 12, 2006.

Here as some of the statistics from Josh McDowell's book about young people, called *The Last Christian Generation* (Holiday, FL: Green Key Books, 2006): 63 percent don't believe that Jesus is the son of the one true God; 51 percent don't believe that Jesus rose from the dead; and 68 percent don't believe that the Holy Spirit is a real entity.

McDowell's findings about churched young people are equally dismal. It has been estimated that between 69 percent and 94 percent of churched youth are leaving the traditional church after high school, and very few are returning. Furthermore, only 33 percent of churched youth have said that the church will play a part in their lives when they leave home.

6. Robert Wuthnow, *After the Baby Boomers*, p. 53.

(*gres to pp 214*)

CHAPTER 10: SHY WITNESSES, DOORKNOB GODS, BAD POLITICS

1. Jan Woodard, "Conference Offers Last Deal for Healthy Church Seminars," March 2, 2007, p. 6.
2. William James. *The Varieties of Religious Experience* (New York: The Modern Library/Random House, 1994).
3. Quoted in Terry Mattingly, "Stalking the Anti-fundamentalist Voter," May 5, 2004.
4. Pew Research Center for the People and the Press. "Trends in Political Values and Core Attitudes, 1987–2007: Political Landscape More Favorable to Democrats," March 22, 2007. http://people-press.org/reports/pdf/312/pdf.
5. Quoted in Charles Lewis, "Ditching God," *National Post,* July 21, 2007.
6. Ross Douthat, "Crises of Faith," *Atlantic Monthly,* July/August 2007.
7. Cal Thomas, "The Legacy of Jerry Falwell," syndicated column, May 17, 2007.
8. Cal Thomas, "Closing One Door, Opening Another," syndicated column, May 3, 2007.
9. Cal Thomas, "What's Faith Got to Do with It?" syndicated column, June 7, 2007.
10. Phyllis Tickle, *God-Talk in America* (New York: Crossroad, 1997).

CHAPTER 11: DIFFERENT STORIES, DIFFERENT IDENTITIES

1. *The Gay Science,* section 125, tr. Walter Kaufmann.

CHAPTER 12: DIFFERENT MORALITY IN THE HEARTLAND

1. Robert Wuthnow, "Living the Question—Evangelical Christianity and Critical Thought," *Cross Currents,* Summer 1990, vol. 40, issue 2, p 160.
2. Robert N. Bellah, Richard Madsen, William M. Sullivan, Ann Swidler, and Steven M. Tipton, *Habits of the Heart: Individualism and Commitment in American Life* (New York: Harper & Row, 1985), p. 221.

CHAPTER 13: NEW FAMILY VALUES

1. Corporal punishment has been at the center of many evangelicals' work against the child welfare system's investigations of child abuse,

which they believe often undercuts parents' rights and discourages spanking. It was also one of the issues that launched psychologist and president of Focus on the Family James Dobson to evangelical fame when he wrote his book of parenting advice, *Dare to Discipline* (Carol Stream, IL: Tyndale House, 1996). In his book *The Strong-Willed Child* (Carol Stream, IL: Tyndale House, 1978), Dobson emphasized the importance of imposing authority: "By learning to yield to the loving authority . . . of his parents, a child learns to submit to other forms of authority which will confront him later in his life—his teachers, school principal, police, neighbors and employers."

2. George Lakoff, *Moral Politics: How Liberals and Conservatives Think*, 2nd ed. (Chicago: University of Chicago Press, 2002).
3. Kinnaman and Lyons, p. 39.
4. Kinnaman and Lyons, *UnChristian*, p. 22.
5. Wuthnow, *After the Baby Boomers*, p. 214.

CHAPTER 14: WHAT HAPPENS NEXT?
1. Quoted in Hannah Elliot, "Red-Letter Christians a Growing Political Force," *Associated Baptist Press*, June 26, 2007.
2. "Worship as Higher Politics," *Christianity Today*, June 23, 2005.
3. Robert Dilday, "Scripture not easy recipe in politics, ethicists say," *Associated Baptist Press*, June 25, 2007.

ACKNOWLEDGMENTS

I am grateful to all the evangelicals and former evangelicals who told me their stories. They took a risk to testify about the truth of their faith. Special thanks to Greg Warner and Carol Childress for sharing their deep knowledge of evangelical matters, and to Dan Pryor, who has helped me in many ways for many years. Jim Henderson inspired and challenged me, often by poking rhetorical sticks at my ideas. I am deeply grateful for his persistence, good humor, and support.

To my editor, Gideon Weil, who can accept a radical change in plans with more grace and speed than any other human being on earth, thank you. Thanks to my agent, Jandy Nelson, whose energy and good spirits never falter no matter the provocation. To Lisa Zuniga and her crew, gratitude for all the ways you saved me.

To my friends and family, thank you. You are more than I deserve. I'll attempt to pick a less trying project in the future.

INDEX > goes to pg. 221 ... (= 5 pp.)

- A -

219.

-K-

-M-(cont.)

— S —(cont)

— The End —